# FROM MOSCOW TO STALINGRAD

## THE EASTERN FRONT, 1941–1942

CASEMATE | ILLUSTRATED

CASEMATE | ILLUSTRATED

# FROM MOSCOW TO STALINGRAD

## THE EASTERN FRONT, 1941–1942

YVES BUFFETAUT

CASEMATE | ILLUSTRATED

MILITARIA

CIS0005

Print Edition: ISBN 978-1-61200-6093
Digital Edition: ISBN 978-1-61200-6109

This book is published in cooperation with and under license from Sophia Histoire & Collections. Originally published in French as Militaria Hors-Serie No 18, © Histoire & Collections 1995


Translation by Hannah McAdams
Design by Paul Hewitt, Battlefield Design
Color illustrations by Jean Restayn © Histoire & Collections
Cartography by Christophe Camilotte © Histoire & Collections
Photo retouching and separations by Remy Spezzano
Additional text by Ruth Sheppard
Printed and bound by Megaprint, Turkey

CASEMATE PUBLISHERS (US)
Telephone (610) 853-9131
Fax (610) 853-9146
Email: casemate@casematepublishers.com
www.casematepublishers.com

CASEMATE PUBLISHERS (UK)
Telephone (01865) 241249
Fax (01865) 794449
Email: casemate-uk@casematepublishers.co.uk
www.casematepublishers.co.uk

Title page: A 37mm anti-aircraft piece positioned to fire against targets on the ground, on the front at Sevastopol in spring 1942. All available artillery was called upon to support the infantry's assaults on the fortress. (Bundesarchiv)

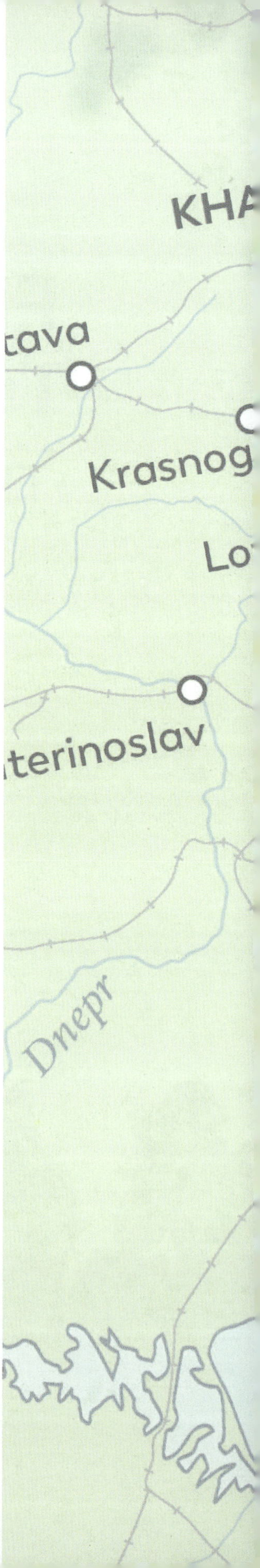

# Contents

# Timeline of Events

The invasion and occupation of the western Soviet Union had long been an ideological aim of the Nazis, and planning for Operation *Barbarossa* began in the summer of 1940. Hitler dismissed concerns about the risks of the plan. He was convinced that the Wehrmacht could achieve victory over the Soviet Union in just a few months. However soon after the invasion began, it became clear that Soviet forces were much stronger than estimated, and German plans would need to change. Hitler began to shape offensive plans to fulfil his new plan, the defeat of the Soviet Union through economic means.

JUN 1941 · JUL · AUG · SEP · OCT · NOV · DEC

**June 22, 1941**
The Germans launch Operation *Barbarossa*, invading the Soviet Union along a 3,000-kilometer front and advancing deep into Soviet territory. The plan called for the capture of the USSR capital Moscow within four months.

**October 13, 1941**
The Germans reach defensive lines outside Moscow, however the battle to take the city stalls as the exhausted German forces suffer logistics and supply issues.

**November 16, 1941**
The Soviets evacuate Kerch Peninsula in the Crimea. German attacks are soon launched against Sevastopol which is the last Soviet stronghold in the Crimea.

**December 5, 1941**
Soviet counteroffensive pushes the German forces back from Moscow, and the Wehrmacht takes up a defensive stance.

**December 26, 1941**
Soviet landings near Kerch. The Soviet offensive continues into March 1942, though they fail to relieve Sevastopol.

Mechanics refuel a Junkers Ju 87 D-1. (Bundesarchiv)

JAN 1942 · FEB · MAR · APR · MAY · JUN · JUL · AUG

**January 8, 1942**
Soviet offensive launched against Kharkov and the upper Donets.

**April 5, 1942**
Hitler issues Directive no. 41 which outlines his planned offensive on the Eastern Front.

**May 8, 1942**
In preparation for new offensive, Germans launch successful preparatory operation against Kerch.

**May 12, 1942**
Soviets launch attack from the Izium salient at Kharkov just as Group von Kleist prepare to launch another preparatory offensive to take the salient. Despite desperate efforts the Russians are defeated with heavy losses.

**June 7, 1942**
Concerted German offensive launched to take Sevastopol. The battle lasts almost a month before the final defenders surrender.

**June 28, 1942**
Case *Blau* is launched.

**July 23, 1942**
Army Group A captures Rostov then pushes into the Caucasus, taking Novorossiysk, the last Soviet naval base on the Black Sea, in early September, but never reaching the Turkish border as planned.

**August 23, 1942**
Soviet forces attack the German bridgehead on the Don but the Germans push ahead to the Volga, north of Stalingrad.

**August 30, 1942**
Army Group B begins advance on Stalingrad.

A heavy Valentine tank captured by German troops in the Crimea, at the beginning of 1942. The hull front has been hit by a missile, almost certainly an 88mm shell, as shown by the extensive damage to the thick armor plating. Its tactical insignia is neatly painted on the turret. (Bundesarchiv)

# The Russian Counteroffensive in the Southern Sector

By early December 1941, the German offensive against Moscow had ground to a halt and ill-equipped German soldiers were struggling simply to survive as the coldest winter of the twentieth century took hold. Marshal Zhukov's massive counteroffensive to remove the threat against the city began slowly but soon began to push back the German line. While Hitler and his generals argued over whether they should withdraw or hold the line, the Soviet offensive paid off, causing considerable German losses.

The conditions of the winter of 1941–42 were so severe that only the most robust aircraft could take to the skies, like these unsophisticated and somewhat elderly Henschel Hs 123 attack biplanes. Their payload was limited to four 50kg bombs, but they could fly in any weather—as long as their motors didn't freeze. In this shot, a mechanic blasts the ventilator of a whitewashed Hs 123 with hot air. (Bundesarchiv)

Zhukov's offensive was not the only movement at this time; there were operations both to the north and south. The operations designed to chase von Leeb from Leningrad will not be dealt with here as the events in the south are of far greater interest when studying the development of the German offensive towards the Caucasus and Stalingrad.

## The German Front in December 1941

At the end of December, Army Group South, too exposed to its front, fell back to the Mius Line where it was able to establish a solid base. In January, the commander of the army group, Field Marshal Walter von Reichenau, suffered a stroke and died during an ill-fated evacuation flight to Germany. He was replaced as commander of the army group by Fedor von Bock, the former commander of Army Group Center, who had just recovered from a stomach ulcer. General Friedrich Paulus had been named head of Sixth Army only a short time before, after Hitler relieved von Rundstedt of his position as commander of Army Group South and promoted von Reichenau to the position. Paulus had spent most of his career as part of the general staff, having commanded nothing larger than an infantry company during the previous war, and an experimental motorized battalion for a few months subsequently. He owed his appointment mostly to the benevolence of General Franz Halder, the chief of Oberkommando des Heeres staff, whose deputy he was, and to von Reichenau himself. The latter accumulated during several weeks the command of Army Group South and that of Sixth Army, after von Rundstedt's retirement.

Paulus in late 1941, Soviet Union. (Bundesarchiv, Bild 101I-021-2081-24A)

## In Profile: Friedrich Paulus

Friedrich Paulus joined the German army in 1910. He saw action during World War I and after the Treaty of Versailles became a career staff officer in the Reichswehr. Clever and hard working, though unsuited to battlefield command, his abilities saw him advance in the peacetime army. When Germany mobilized for war in 1939 he was made chief of staff for the Tenth (later Sixth) Army. In September 1940 he became deputy chief of the General Staff for operations, conducting studies for the invasion of the Soviet Union.

In late 1941, having never commanded a unit larger than a battalion, he was made commander of Sixth Army. The following summer his army led the drive on Stalingrad. By November, Sixth Army was surrounded by an entire Soviet army group, but Paulus, convinced of Hitler's military genius, followed his orders to hold his position. Von Manstein came to relieve him, but Paulus would not break out without orders. The order never came. The Sixth Army fought on for two more months until finally, on 31 January 1943, Paulus surrendered, just hours after he had been promoted to field marshal by Hitler. Hitler had expected him to commit suicide as no German field marshal had ever been taken alive.

As a high-ranking officer, he was useful as a propaganda tool, and the Soviet authorities persuaded him to make anti-Nazi broadcasts. He gave testimony at the Nuremburg trials against both Keitel and Jodl. He was kept in captivity until 1953, dying in East Germany four years later.

At the end of 1941, Army Group South, consisting of 37 German divisions and seven allied divisions, was arranged from north to south as follows: Second Army (von Weichs) between Kursk and Orel; Sixth Army (Paulus) in the Kharkov area; Seventeenth Army (Hoth) on the upper course of the Donets; and First Panzer Army (von Kleist) by the Azov Sea. These units were supported by Air Fleet 4, which comprised around 300 operational aircraft, mostly bombers.

## The Soviets attack

In front of Army Group South was the Soviet Southwestern Front, commanded by Marshal Semyon Timoshenko, with Ivan Bagramyan as chief of staff and Nikita Khrushchev as political commissar. The Soviet units were arranged from north to south as follows:

- the Bryansk Front (Cherevichenko): 3rd, 13th and 61st Armies, south of Toula;
- the Southwestern Front (Kostenko): 40th, 21st, 38th and 6th Armies;
- the Southern Front (Malinovsky): 57th, 9th, 37th, 12th, 18th and 56th Armies.

Another shot of a Henschel Hs 123, taken around the same time. This one has not been painted white, so presents a clear target against the snow. Two mechanics appear to be puzzling over the aircraft's motor. The engine cowling of the Henschel Hs 123, composed of three elements, could be easily removed, allowing exceptional access to the powertrain. This photograph shows the robustness of the aircraft's landing gear, a huge advantage when landing on icy runways. (Bundesarchiv)

The first attacks involved the Bryansk Front, with two armies coming from the Southwestern Front (the 40th and the 21st). Their objective was to retake Orel and Kursk, but progress was minimal and the front of the German Second Army was unbroken.

On January 18, a bigger offensive, of five armies, was directed against Kharkov and especially against the upper Donets, in the direction of Dnipropetrovsk. The Seventeenth Army suffered the initial shock, as did the southern wing of Sixth Army. The fighting was brisk, and the Germans were outnumbered: seven infantry divisions faced 21 infantry divisions, 11 cavalry divisions, and 10 armored brigades. The result was a breach 120 kilometers wide in the German front, and on January 26, the Russians had advanced over 100 kilometers beyond it. On that day, the mobile elements seized Lozovaya, the main logistical center of the Seventeenth Army, which was almost completely destroyed. As a result, von Bock united the First Panzer Army and Seventeenth Army to form Army Group Kleist; and created Group von Mackensen with 3rd Panzer Group, in order to consolidate the left wing of the Seventeenth Army. This allowed the Germans to stabilize the front and take back some of the land they had lost, notably the length of the Samara River. When the battle ended, the Russians retained a salient towards Kursk and Kharkov, and most importantly towards a bridgehead at the North Donets, which allowed them to threaten Kharkov and the Dnieper.

# The Front at Sevastopol

On October 31, 1941, the Russian front on the Crimean Peninsula had been ruptured by the Germans; part of the 51st Army fell back to the Kerch Peninsula. During the weeks that followed, XXXXII Army Corps pushed the Soviets back as far as Kerch, which was evacuated on November 16 following the abandonment of all heavy weaponry. The infantry crossed across the 10-kilometer stretch of sea to the Kuban, Taman Peninsula.

The only Russian defenders in the Crimea were therefore entrenched in Sevastopol, the command of which was placed in the hands of naval commander Admiral Filip Oktyabrsky. Sevastopol was defended by three concentric defensive lines over 16 km deep. The artillery had around 170 guns, some of which were emplaced in concrete bunkers. The garrison of the fortress was boosted by the arrival of Petrov's Independent Coastal Army, evacuated from Odessa, and by a substantial number of men, transferred by the fleet from the Kuban. Oktyabrsky then had 52,000 men at his disposal to defend Sevastopol.

An SdKfz 11 traverses a ruined village during the winter of 1941–42. Despite climatic and strategic conditions, the men on board are still smiling. A whitewash has been applied over the panzer-gray paint, and the engine cowling has been covered in straw. (Bundesarchiv)

Sevastopol was valuable as both a naval and air base. Sited on a promontory, it was hazardous for an enemy to approach by land; the high cliffs protecting the harbor made amphibious landings equally treacherous. The Soviet navy had enhanced these natural defences, installing 188mm and 305mm naval guns able to fire both out to sea and inland and protected by reinforced concrete bunkers.

Erich von Manstein wanted to seize the port before the end of the year and tested the Russian defenses in November by engaging LIV Army Corps. This was clearly insufficient, and it soon became apparent that only a full offensive would be able to overwhelm it. Preparations were difficult, as recent heavy rain meant that the roads were full of holes. In addition, the harsh winter in Ukraine had totally disrupted the railroad system and supplies, as well as reinforcements, hadn't shown up. Finally, the Romanian troops were occupied by resistance fighters in the Yalta sector, which reduced further the number of units that could be engaged against Sevastopol.

Finally, on December 17, the 22nd and 132nd Infantry Divisions attacked to the north of the town, along the Baalbek Valley, while to the south of Sevastopol, the 24th and 50th Infantry Divisions tried to seize heights that overlooked the port. The battle was particularly tough. Although there were initial successes, during the prolonged fighting, the influence of the NKVD and the political commissars—who would not tolerate failure—strengthened and the resistance became fierce. Von Choltitz, commander of the 22nd Infantry Division, noted in his memoirs that if the Russian defense had become desperate, his losses would have been enormous. The 16th Infantry Regiment, however, soon arrived near the northern bay of Sevastopol. To the south, less progress was made, as the Soviet lines were protected by barbed wire and casemates, though it seemed that the Russian front was on the verge of collapse.

The Soviet landing on the Kerch Peninsula surprised the Germans and forced them to cede ground. However, in part due to the difficult weather conditions, the action was not a total success. This impressive shot shows a heavy landing craft stranded on a beach. Its load of trucks was destroyed. This vessel is very similar to barges built by the British and Americans. (Bundesarchiv)

Another view of the same scene, with a gutted Stuart and two turrets in the foreground. A half-burned speedboat shell can be seen in the background. The landing barge is the same as that in the previous shot, confirmed by the presence of the destroyed truck at the top of the ramp, next to an antiaircraft piece. Following the terrible losses of summer 1941, the Soviet armored forces had, in 1942, many British and American tanks at their disposal, including Valentines, Matildas, Stuarts, and Grant/Lees. (Bundesarchiv)

Several M3 Stuart tanks destroyed during an engagement inland. This photo was taken several months after the battle, in spring (the trees are in flower), when the Crimea was retaken by von Manstein. (Bundesarchiv)

Two impressive shots of a Russian battleship taken under Luftwaffe fire. It resembles a ghost ship returned from the battle of Tsushima in May 1905, when Admiral Rozhestvensky's imperial Russian fleet was wiped out by Admiral Togo's Japanese squadron. This vessel was obviously abandoned and used for target practice by the Luftwaffe. The exact identity of the ship is unknown, as its superstructures have been remodeled, but it appears to date from the end of the 19th century or early 20th. (Bundesarchiv)

The reaction of the Stavka, the Red Army's general staff, was immediate—Admiral Oktyabrsky ordered a retreat to the Trans-Caucasian Front at Kozlov, in the Kuban. He sent an infantry division and a naval infantry brigade to Sevastopol as reinforcements on December 21, as part of the Black Sea Fleet came to defend the fortress with artillery. But in that case that proved insufficient, two landings were organized on the Kerch Peninsula, in difficult weather and with little support, by groups of paratroopers dropped to the rear of the enemy. The 51st Army landed 13,000 men on December 26 near Kerch, while 3,000 men of the 44th Army arrived on Cape Opuk.

The Germans had only General von Sponeck's 46th Infantry Division to face this huge Russian landing. Von Sponeck asked von Manstein for authorization to retreat behind the Ak Monai strait, allowing him to shorten the lines by abandoning the Kerch Peninsula. Von Manstein refused.

On December 29, 23,000 Russian soldiers landed near Theodosia, with the aim of cutting the 46th Infantry Division's lines of communication. This operation, along with the fact that the Azov Sea was freezing over, allowing Soviet troops to cross on foot, incited

An old Russian battleship lists and begins to sink following a bomb impact. Despite the aerial superiority of the Germans, the Axis forces never gained control over the Black Sea, and were unable to bring in any large tonnage ships because of the strict neutrality of the Turks, which forbade passage to all belligerents through the Bosporus. (Bundesarchiv)

von Sponeck to order his division to retreat regardless of von Manstein's previous refusal, abandoning guns and other heavy armaments as they did so. This decision was without doubt the only feasible one, as the Romanian units, notably the mountain troops, sent to Theodosia by von Manstein, retreated as soon as they encountered the Red Army.

The risk of the collapse of the Eastern Front at Crimea forced von Manstein to suspend his attack on Sevastopol, even though it was going well for the Germans. He sent the 132nd and 170th Infantry Divisions to help the Romanians; they, in doing so, retook Theodosia. But it was too late for the Germans, as the Azov Sea was now totally frozen over and the Russian

A PzKpfw III at the beginning of 1942. It bears the figure "372" on the base of its turret, replicated on one of the replacement rollers at the back of the vehicle. A tactical insignia is painted on the gun barrel, which is unusual: it belongs to the unit's general staff. (Bundesarchiv)

troops no longer needed ships to cross it. The situation was critical. Von Sponeck was not only relieved of command, but also court martialled and condemned to death. Just days later Erich Hoepner would withdraw his forces outside Moscow on his own initiative to prevent huge losses and would be treated similarly. Von Sponeck's death sentence was commuted, and he was finally executed without trial in July 1944, after the attempt on Hitler's life.

In January and February 1942, the Soviet offensive continued without abatement, though the Russians were still unable to relieve Sevastopol. On March 13, a new effort—with eight infantry divisions and two armored brigades—failed within three days, the Soviets leaving behind 130 tanks as they fled. On March 20, von Manstein counterattacked with the 22nd Panzer Division, as yet inexperienced in combat. It showed—the attack failed.

The fierce pursuit of their counteroffensive caused the Soviets such heavy losses at the beginning of 1942 that, by spring, the Wehrmacht found itself once again in a state of materiel superiority. Certainly, the Russians still had a considerable number of tanks, but the units were disorganized and unprepared for combat. On the other side, the Heer had new materiel, such as this Sturmgeschütz 40 Ausf. F of which the first examples appeared in 1942. (Bundesarchiv)

# | The Wehrmacht Prepares

**The 1942 German offensive is of upmost importance in the history of World War II, as it was the first entirely directed by Adolf Hitler himself, after von Brauchitsch's dismissal during the battle of Moscow.**

The undeniable success of the defensive battle fought during the winter after the defeat outside Moscow convinced Hitler that he had a greater gift for the art of war than any—or indeed all—of his generals. Naming himself commander-in-chief of the Heer (German army), the Führer totally transformed the way the general staff worked. The time for testing future operations through *Kriegsspiel* (simulations or war games) was over—from now on, the Führer would give precise orders that the army were obligated to carry out. Nonetheless, the generals continued to attempt to influence Hitler's decisions.

In January 1942, morale within the OKH was at its lowest. It was at this time that General Günther Blumentritt (so useful to historians thanks to his extensive memoirs) joined the Heer's general staff, replacing Paulus. He wrote:

Kharkov was the objective of General Timoshenko, who wanted to beat the Germans by attacking first. (Bundesarchiv)

> **Several generals have declared that relaunching the offensive in 1942 is impossible, and that it would be wiser to guard properly that which has already been won. Halder was very hesitant on this question of resuming the offensive. Von Rundstedt was much more categoric and strongly advised that the German army retreat to the bases in Poland. Von Leeb agreed with him. Without committing themselves to such a radical solution, a lot of the generals worried where such a campaign would lead … But with the departure of von Rundstedt and that of Brauchitsch, the resistance to Hitler's pressure—the pressure to resume the offensive—weakened considerably.**

The departure of Generals Gerd von Rundstedt and Walter von Brauchitsch did indeed impact the remaining generals' resistance to the Führer, but it was not the only factor: the failure of the Soviet counteroffensive to crush the Heer surely had an influence too.

## The Priorities of the German Generals

It is often said that history is written by the victors. Yet this is only partially true; it might be more accurate to say that history is written by the survivors. In the case of World War II in general and the German army in particular, the survivors were the generals who, in their memoirs, criticized Hitler relentlessly (a task made immeasurably easier by his death) to distance themselves from the Nazi regime after its true nature was revealed in 1945.

In 1941 and 1942, when Hitler took definitive control over the armed forces, it could be said that he had an altogether clearer vision for them than did their generals. The latter, after their misadventure in Moscow, advocated a strategy of limited objectives, aiming towards the defeat of the Red Army, but not to conquer the Soviet Union completely—that would be far too risky. However, the United States' entry into the war meant that the Axis forces had to act quickly, before the now strengthened Allies made any chance of success impossible. This the Japanese admirals understood in 1942, when they tried several times to stop the

American fleet in the Pacific. Hitler was on the same page when he decided to launch a new general offensive in the East, to defeat the Red Army, to conquer the oil fields in the Caucasus and to crush the USSR, after which he would—as he told his generals—turn his attention westwards.

The German generals did not seem to have major strategic views; they were obsessed with the balance of forces in the East. It's fair to say this was not very encouraging, but once again, when Germany re-engaged on the Russian Front, the armed forces had no choice but to win quickly or lose everything.

In November 1941, the OKH intelligence service, directed by Eberhard Kinzel, indicated that contrary to previous reports, the Red Army, by May 1942, would be able to re-equip no fewer than 150 infantry divisions, 30 cavalry divisions, and several armored formations, who would be given British and American tanks. In December, Kinzel estimated the number of infantry divisions facing the Wehrmacht in Russia at 200, not including the 40 armored brigades and 35 cavalry divisions. The Germans were evidently surprised by the Russians' ability to rebuild and rearm.

This did not give Halder, chief of staff of the Heer, much confidence and he—as he had the previous year—butted heads with Hitler several times. Before a definitive decision was made, the two men came to an agreement on two preliminary operations: first, the retaking of the Kerch Peninsula and the capture of Sevastopol, and second, the reduction of the Izium salient threatening Kharkov.

General von Manstein commanded the Eleventh Army in the Crimea, with remarkable success. He swept through the peninsula before attacking the fortress of Sevastopol. He is pictured here, in the center of this photograph, with his left hand on his knee, during the siege of the port. Von Manstein was called upon to take an increasingly important role on the Eastern Front after the disaster at Stalingrad. (Bundesarchiv)

The Germans used many large flat-bottomed barges on the Crimean Front. Each was equipped with powerful Flak canons. (Bundesarchiv)

Two typical ships from the German flotilla in the Black Sea: on the right, an R-Boat alongside a *Fährpram*. Very large and thus very stable, the *Fährpram* carried an important load. (Bundesarchiv)

Romanian and German troops land on the Kerch Peninsula. The soldiers in the foreground are from Romania; those from Germany are on the *Fährpram* behind. (Bundesarchiv)

## Success at Kerch

The first of Germany's preliminary operations was undertaken against Kerch. Von Manstein's Eleventh Army managed to regroup six German divisions and three Romanian divisions for the attack; the Luftwaffe in the sector was reinforced by Richthofen's VIII Air Corps, bringing the totals to 11 *Kampfgeschwader* (bomber), three *Stukageschwader* and seven *Jagdgeschwader* (fighter) wings.

The Russians were far greater in number, and had lined up three armies—the 44th, the 47th, and the 51st—but their defenses lacked depth, and their first line was crushed by aviation and artillery on the first day of the assault, May 8, 1942. The first breach was only five kilometers wide, but the Soviets were unable to close it, and the Germans got a foothold to their rear thanks to the surprise arrival of light armored elements.

On May 12, the battle was virtually won, and on the 15th, the Germans entered Kerch. Some Russian soldiers were able to flee to the Kuban, but they left behind all their equipment, and the spoils were considerable: 170,000 prisoners, 1,100 guns, 250 tanks, 3,800 trucks, and 300 planes.

The Germans only lost 7,500 men and the Russians had shown a great tactical weakness, the defenders at Sevastopol remaining inert despite only facing second-order Romanian troops. It is interesting that at around the same time, on the northern front, a Russian offensive launched by two Siberian divisions commanded by General Andrey Vlasov, considered by Stalin to be one of his best generals, ended in bitter failure due to a lack of reserves and the obstinacy of the Stavka in ordering the offensive to continue when all was lost. Vlasov was surrounded and refused to get on the aircraft that would save him, as he would not abandon his men. Held prisoner with his general staff, he ended up defecting to the enemy and established an army of volunteers allied to Germany, the so-called 'Russian Liberation Army'.

Operations on the Kerch Peninsula. In the foreground, a 105mm howitzer unloaded by the FH 18 a little earlier. In the background are several *Fährpram*, various ships and an R-Boot. (Bundesarchiv)

*Below:* Ships of all types were used to land the last of the Russian troops. On the left is a real landing barge; on the right, a Danube pleasure cruiser looking rather the worse for wear. (Bundesarchiv)

This T-34/76 lost during Timoshenko's offensive against Kharkov doesn't appear to be damaged, at least from this angle. It could have been abandoned due to a breakdown, as suggested by the oil slick in front of the right track. (Bundesarchiv)

## Timoshenko Strikes First at Kharkov

The second German offensive—*Fredericus I*—aimed at the reabsorption of the Izium salient. It was an operation of considerable scope, launched by Group von Kleist, comprising the First Panzer Army and Hoth's Seventeenth Army. But events overtook them: the Southwestern Front attacked on May 12 with substantial force, 23 infantry divisions, two cavalry divisions and two armored brigades charged the 11 divisions of Paulus's Sixth Army, in the direction of Kharkov.

The Russian general had committed a terrible error in his choice of starting line: he had amassed his armored units in the Izium salient, the exact place at which von Kleist was directing his concentric attack. This would have profound consequences.

On May 12, the Soviets attacked the front of Sixth Army, where the fighting immediately became fierce. However, the Russians easily pushed forward from the Izium salient, where around 600 tanks destroyed the German front, held by the Romanians. They then thrust towards Krasnogrod, moving over 100 kilometers to threaten Kharkov from the south. But the Soviet corridor lacked width, as in the north Paulus's Sixth Army had lost ground, but retreated and re-established itself on the Belgorod–Kharkov railroad. All Russian attempts to drive them out were unsuccessful.

The losses suffered by Timoshenko during the advance on Kharkov were tragic on the eve of the German offensive. This photograph shows four T-34s and a light T-60 tank destroyed on the outskirts of a town. (Bundesarchiv)

To the south, the situation was even more dangerous, as the Russian units came up against Group von Kleist. Timoshenko understood that the remarkable advance in the central sector of his attack front threatened disaster if his flanks could not be strengthened and if the enemy succeeded in counterattacking at the base of the salient. During the night of May 17/18, he called the Stavka to warn them of the situation. Stalin didn't want to respond, and told him to continue his offensive on Kharkov. In his memoirs, Khrushchev indicates that when he was political commissar for Timoshenko, he had tried to annul Stalin's order, but this claim should be treated with some caution—Khrushchev, after all, was one of the "survivors" writing after the event.

*Rasputitsa* is the Russian term for the season when travel on unpaved roads became difficult due to the spring thaw or autumn rains. Moving armies during the muddy season was extremely problematic, as Napoleon discovered, and it repeatedly slowed or stopped operations during fighting on the Eastern Front during World War II. In May 1942, the mud caused severe delays to Soviet preparations in the Izium salient.

The losses caused by Timoshenko's divisions' deep advance into Kharkov were greatest among the German units surprised by the Soviets far behind the front. This burnt-out half-track, beside a crushed 50mm Pak gun, is an SdKfz 10 or Zgkw 1-tonne Typ D7. (Bundesarchiv)

On May 17, 1942, III Panzer Corps, consisting of two panzer divisions and a motorized division, supporting eight German infantry divisions and four Romanian divisions, attacked the southern flank of the Izium salient. The 9th and 57th Soviet Armies attempted to fend them off, but were quickly separated from each other. By the end of the first day, the Germans had penetrated 40 kilometers into the enemy lines, and the next day Izium was captured, and the Russian salient, at this point over 120 km deep, risked being cut off in a matter of hours. Timoshenko once again called on the Stavka to stop the offensive towards Kharkov, hoping to save what he still could. But Stalin remained intractable, and the ensuing counterattack with Timoshenko leading the 5th Cavalry Corps failed.

On May 19, the order from Moscow finally arrived—but it was too late. General Gorodnyaski, who commanded the armored vehicles engaged at Kharkov, tried to continue towards the city to thrust northwards and rejoin the troops of 6th Army. He never arrived. Timoshenko then sent General Kostenko, his adjutant, into the pocket to organize the breakthrough of the 6th and 9th Soviet Armies. They did succeed, albeit partially—one-quarter of the two armies made it through. The Russian defeat was complete.

The Germans had lost 20,000 men while the Russians counted 5,000 dead, 70,000 MIA, and 300 tanks lost. According to the *Kriegstagebuch des OKW*, the Soviets had in fact lost 214,000 prisoners, 2,000, guns and 1,200 tanks. This last figure is clearly exaggerated: Timoshenko only had 845 tanks at the beginning of the offensive.

Whatever the losses might have been, the consequences of this unfortunate offensive were dire for the Red Army. It appears almost certain that Timoshenko's attack was launched,

German Offensives, May 1942
Tula
BRYANSK FRONT
Bryansk
Orel
Tambov
Penza
Second Panzer Army
40th Army
Second Army
Kursk
Voronezh
Saratov
21st Army
Fourth Panzer Army
SOUTHWESTERN FRONT
28th Army
Second Army
HONG
Kharkov
Don
38th Army
Sixth Army
Dnepr
6th Army
37th Army
Stalingrad
Ekaterinoslav
56th Army
51st Army
First Panzer Army
18th Army
26th Army
Volga
Seventeenth Army
Rostov
17th Army
Eleventh Army
Kertch
Sevastopol
Krasnodar
Voroshilovsk
Novorossisk
47th Army
Tuapse
Sochi
Grozny
BLACK SEA
Batoum
Tiflis
Front line 1 May 1942
German advance
Samsun
Trabzon
TRANS-CAUCASIAN FRONT
0 50 100 250 km

This convoy of Russian trucks was surprised while crossing a ford over a wide but shallow river. The radiators of these GAZ trucks have been peppered with bullets. (Bundesarchiv)

under orders from Stalin, to destroy the German forces preparing for the inevitable summer offensive; the capture of Kharkov was only therefore a secondary objective. After the war, the Germans declared that Timoshenko's attack had had a negligible effect on the Heer. But its effects had been catastrophic for the Soviets, who had lost their best elements on the eve of the large German offensive.

## The Last of the Preliminary Offensives

Before the general attack towards the East, the Germans had to rectify their front in two places: first, they had to reduce the Volchansk salient, and second, they needed to create a bridgehead on the east bank of the Oskol, a tributary of the Donets. Operation *Wilhelm* was launched on June 10 by Sixth Army against the 28th Soviet Army in the Volchansk area. This time, the Russians did not make the same mistake they had at Kharkov, and immediately retreated 50 km. Still, they left behind them 40,000 men who were taken prisoner. On June 15, the battle ended.

It was reprised from June 22 to 26, under the operation name *Fredericus II*, with the First Panzer Army and part of Paulus's army advancing in the direction of Koupiansk, across the Oskol. There too, the Germans experienced success on contact. The Southwestern Front was exhausted on the eve of the grand German offensive.

Russian villagers move amongst three destroyed KV-1s in a Ukrainian field during Timoshenko's offensive against Kharkov. The ground must have been fairly wet, as the tanks' tracks are filled with mud and straw. The top of the turret in the foreground has been covered in white paint. (Bundesarchiv)

A scene of disaster for British equipment: in a marshy zone, several British infantry tanks have become bogged down and destroyed by artillery or demolition teams. Among them are three Valentines and, in the center, a Matilda II missing its turret. This photo was taken from too great a distance for the inscriptions to be completely legible; however, the numbers 20 and 21 are visible, having been painted on in haste either by the Russians, or by the Germans keeping count of enemy losses. One of the Valentines has a star on its turret. (Bundesarchiv)

# In Profile:
# Allied Tanks in Soviet Service, and PaK 40

Large numbers of Valentine tanks were used by the Red Army. The markings on the profile image are taken from a tank caught on film at the time. As for all Soviet "documentaries" of World War II, it is best taken with a pinch of salt—they were often only made after the war had already ended.

The 7.5cm Pak 40 heavy anti-tank gun "learnt the ropes" during the battle of Kharkov, in May 1942. The gun did, however, arrive late, the 3.7 and 5cm guns proving inefficient in the face of the T-34 and other KV-1s. With this gun, the Germans finally had at their disposal a high-performance anti-tank gun, capable of puncturing 132mm of armor at 500 meters, marking a tremendous progression from the 36mm at 500 meters that marked the upper limits of anti-tank capability at the beginning of the conflict.

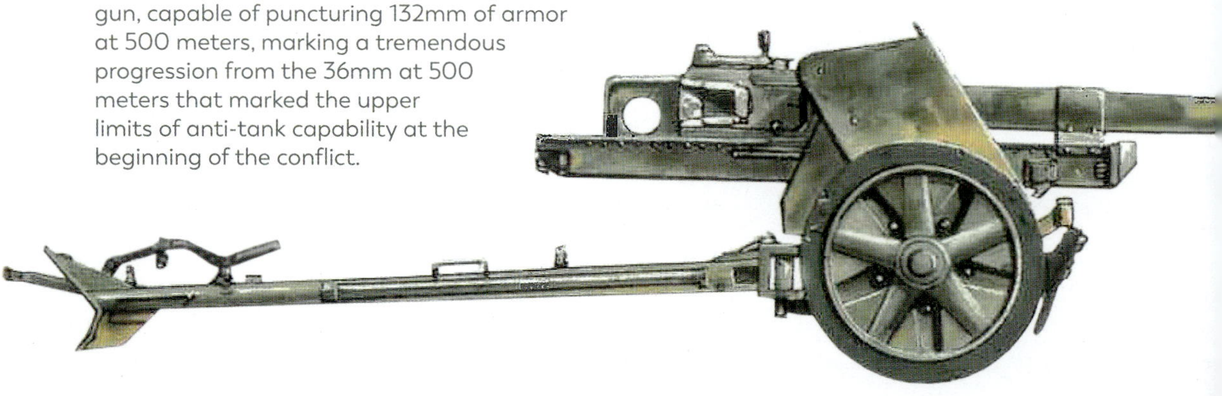

A Soviet Lee tank on the Southern Front during the summer of 1942. There were a large number of British and American-built tanks in the Red Army in 1942—particularly on the Southern Front, not only because it was deemed the most important due to the German offensive, but also because Allied materiel could get to the Soviet Union through Iran. This tank bears a simple star as a mark of nationality. Some Lee tanks still bore their American serial numbers. (Bundesarchiv)

*Right:* The insignia of a Pak company, 13th Panzer Division. For obvious reasons of discretion, German artillerymen avoided affixing any type of tactical mark to their anti-tank pieces. On the other hand, these insignias were visible on tractors. However, all rules have their exception, and we do find tactical signs, victory markings (in the form of white circles), and names given to the pieces or other personal insignias painted on their barrels.

All allies of Germany served on the Southern Front—with the obvious exception of Finland. In this shot, Romanian officers are watching with interest an SdKfz 221 recon vehicle modified to carry a 2.8cm sPzB 41 anti-tank gun. This was an incredible gun, with a bore that tapered from 28mm at the breech to 20mm at the mouth. This squeezed the shell, improving flight characteristics and increasing its initial velocity, meaning that shells fired from this gun had the potential to pierce 50mm of armor at 500 meters. This made the sPzB 41 superior to the Pak 36/37. (Bundesarchiv)

At the same time, Paulus made the headlines, as Walter Görlitz wrote:

> **The battle of Kharkov earned Paulus the Knight's Cross, a distinction that, at the time, had not had the same abusive usage as in the final years of the war. His name was cited in the press. For a brief time, he became some sort of warhorse for National-Socialist propaganda, as had Rommel before him. Paulus received the congratulations of the generals who barely knew his name, of distant relatives who never turned up: from childhood friends of his sister to Romanian cousins of his wife. Photographs of him appeared in all the newspapers.**[1]

This celebration of Paulus would have unfortunate repercussions the following year.

1 Walter Gorlitz, *Stalingrad, vie du generalfeldmarschall Frederic Paulus* (Paris: Fayard, 1962), p. 89.

An Italian speedboat on the Black Sea. From the reduced size of its engine, we can guess that this is an MTSM, 8.4 meters long and carrying, aside from its two-man crew, an armament consisting of two depth charges, visible on the port side, and a 450mm torpedo. Over 100 speedboats of this type were built between 1941 and 1943. It was on a larger MAS-type speedboat that von Manstein narrowly escaped death during the siege of Sevastopol. (Bundesarchiv)

## The Eleventh Army in Crimea

At the end of May, all eyes turned towards the Crimea, where General von Manstein would attempt to capture the fortress of Sevastopol before crossing the Kerch strait to the Kuban, to take back the Russian defenses of the Caucasus.

At Sevastopol, the Soviet garrison was more powerful than it had been in December 1941, though the meteorological conditions were now less favorable towards the Russians. They had seven infantry divisions, three naval infantry brigades, and a number of improvised units, notably including civilians. Finally, two supplementary infantry brigades landed

A convoy of Büssing-NAG trucks in the Crimea. The heavy vehicles carry their name in relief on their bumpers, which is somewhat original. If is therefore possible to make out that this type of heavy truck—the 4 x 2 s Lkw 4.5 tonne Type 500 s, according to Heer terminology—was equipped with a six-cylinder diesel engine (6 ZYL—Diesel). (Bundesarchiv)

at Sevastopol during the battle. In total, this amounted to 70 battalions. According to the "official" Soviet history, the garrison had at their disposal over 600 guns and 40 tanks.

On the German side, LIV Army Corps attacked to the north, XXX Army Corps to the south, and the Romanian mountain troops in the center. This amounted to seven German infantry divisions and two Romanian infantry divisions.

Von Manstein had no tanks, but instead several Sturmgeschütz units and some Goliath vehicles tasked with bombing the enemy bunkers. His artillery comprised 700 guns and howitzers and a number of heavy mortars. Paul Carell estimated it at 1,300 artillery pieces in total.[2]

The Luftwaffe had an aerial corps in place—the VIII Air Corps—with seven bomber wings, three Stuka wings and four fighter wings, as well as 17 heavy Flak batteries.

The sky was therefore the only domain in which the Germans had numerical superiority. On the ground, the assailants faced a difficult challenge as the Soviet defenders were very well entrenched and the terrain they defended was at times so difficult to access that the Sturmgeschütz could not be used.

2 Paul Carell, *Opération Barbarossa* (Paris: Robert Laffont, 1964).

As in all siege warfare, artillery played a key role at Sevastopol. In this photograph, German soldiers witness the shelling of a Soviet position from their trench. Note the helmet coverings marked with white on the rear. (Bundesarchiv)

The cameraman of a propaganda company captures the entry of a Heer armored vehicle through the defenses of Sevastopol. This vehicle is none other than a small, tracked Renault UE, returned to service under German colors. The materiel recuperated in France was indispensable to the German effort in Russia. (Bundesarchiv)

One of 40 Russian tanks from the Sevastopol garrison, destroyed at the bottom of a trench. It is an old T-26, veteran of the fighting in summer 1941. (Bundesarchiv)

These Romanian machine gunners, engaged in the fight for Sevastopol, do not exactly seem enthused about their situation. Germany's allies engaged in the fighting in Russia reluctantly, and their lack of motivation had extreme consequences. (Bundesarchiv)

The battle could have started disastrously for the Germans, as several days before the assault began, von Manstein narrowly escaped death when an Italian speedboat from which he was observing the coast was surprised by Soviet aircraft and shot at. Several men were killed on board, including the speedboat driver and von Manstein's personal chauffeur.

## The Assault on Sevastopol

Over the course of several days, Richthofen's aerial corps and the artillery crushed the Russian positions. For the first time, the Nebelwerfers were used in bulk, with no fewer than 21 batteries. The Germans also had three super-heavy mortars: *Gamma* (427mm caliber), *Karl* (615mm) and the monstrous *Dora* (800mm).

The Russians had established their defenses on three levels. The first constituted a line of trenches and barbed wire, protected by a vast number of mines. The second was a succession of forts and fieldworks, to which the Germans gave names: Molotov, Stalin, GPU, Cheka, Siberia, Volga, Ural etc. To the south of the front were Maxim Gorky II and

# In Profile:
# German Aircraft

The insignia of the 3./StG 2 *Immelmann.*

A Junkers 87 D1 Stuka of the 3./StG 2 *Immelmann*. At this time, the Stuka no longer played a significant role as a dive bomber; however, it became (after some modification) an excellent tank fighter. Like the Stormovik, its Russian counterpart, the Stuka often surprised Soviet fighter planes launched in its pursuit, the latter underestimating the former's defensive capacity.

The famous Henschel 123 ("Eins, zwei, drei"). It was one of the only planes with enough power to tear itself out of the Soviet mud on take-off. Even in 1942, it was still so highly regarded that von Richthofen demanded its return to production, albeit in vain.

An Avia B 534 in Slovak use during the fighting in the Caucasus. The Slovaks sent three squadrons to the Russian Front: the 11th, the 12th, and the 13th. The first two received Messerschmitt Bf 109 Es in October 1942 to replace their outdated biplanes. The 13th Squadron continued to fight with their Avias until the summer of 1943, the letter M being the 13th letter of the alphabet, one can extrapolate that the 11th Squadron used the letter K and the 12th, L.

Two formidable 305mm guns at the Maxim Gorky fortress. (Bundesarchiv)

the fortress Balaclava, which evokes the Crimean War of 1853–56; von Manstein would have studied in detail the history of the French and British campaign against the troops of Tsar Nicholas I.

On June 7, 1942, a decisive assault was launched. The shock troops set off from their starting line at 0350 hrs. The principal effort was fixed on the north. Four divisions attacked the front in this sector: 22nd, 24th, 50th, and 132nd Infantry Divisions. The infantrymen were supported by the 190th and 249th Sturmgeschütz Battalions. The struggle for the Stalin fort was particularly severe. It was defended by the members of the Komsomol and Communist party who refused to surrender. The war diary of 22nd Infantry Division noted that "They were the toughest adversaries we had ever faced."

Paul Carell gives an example of the ferocious fighting:

> In a blockhouse where a shell had hit, there were 30 dead. Ten survivors fought like the devil. They were blind to the murder and to the bodies of their comrades. "Pioneers", the Germans called them. Flame-throwers spewed their flames against this terrible rampart of bodies. Then came the hand grenades. Infantrymen were vomiting. It was only during the afternoon that four trembling Russians, completely out of ammo, staggered out of the rubble. They surrendered, but the political commissar fired a bullet into each of their heads.[3]

3 Paul Carell, *Opération Barbarossa* (Paris: Robert Laffont, 1964), p. 442.

Von Manstein (right) examining a map with von Richthofen during operations on the Kerch Peninsula, May 1942. (Bundesarchiv, Bild 183-B18921)

## In Profile: Erich von Manstein

In stark contrast to Paulus, von Manstein was probably the most talented German field commander during World War II.

Von Manstein joined the army as a young man and fought during World War I. When Germany invaded Poland in 1939, he was chief of staff to Army Group South, and masterminded the strategy for the invasion of France. He led an infantry corps during the invasion, and was promoted to general. He commanded LVI Panzer Corps during the invasion of the Soviet Union and nearly captured Leningrad. Seen by the Soviets as their greatest opponent, as commander of Eleventh Army he took nearly half a million Soviet prisoners, and captured Sevastopol in July 1942. He almost managed to relieve the Sixth Army at Stalingrad, and a few months later inflicted a massive defeat on the Red Army at Kharkov. He was one of the commanders at the massive tank battle of Kursk.

Von Manstein was dismissed from command in March 1944 after he ordered endangered units to retreat without waiting for permission from Hitler. He was taken prisoner by the British in the summer of 1945. He gave testimony at Nuremburg, but was found guilty of war crimes himself in 1949. He later served as a military advisor to the West German government.

On the German side, too, the losses were heavy: within the two battalions of the 16th Infantry Regiment that took part in the assault against fort Stalin, all the officers were killed.

The battle for the second Russian line, the most solid, had not ended by June 17. Due to their losses, the Bavarian 132nd Infantry Division was withdrawn from battle and replaced by the 24th Infantry Division, which was in turn relieved by the 4th Romanian Mountain Division. The fort Maxim Gorky I, armed with 305mm guns, was still not defeated and the intervention of two heavy 355mm mortars, installed with great difficulty in the Belbek Valley, was needed to silence it for good. However, the Germans still had to defeat the defenders—about 1,000 of them—to which end they employed dynamite, flame-throwers, smoke bombs, and phosphorus. Even after direct hits from Stukas it took several more hours to fight through the corridors of the fort and destroy, one by one, the Russian bastions, whose combatants were equipped with gas masks. By the end of the day, the German pathfinders had reached the heart of the fortress, close to the command center where the final few defenders had gathered. They had been ordered to fight to the death. These were the final radio messages received from Maxim Gorky at the admiralty command center in Sevastopol:

> We are now 46. The Germans are hammering on the armored doors and we shout and we surrender. We have opened the trap to fire twice. That has now become impossible.
>
> We are 21. We are preparing to jump. We are ending transmission. Farewell.

Of 1,000 defenders, the Germans took just 40 as prisoners. Once Maxim Gorky I fell, it took just a few days to roll up the other forts. The Germans arrived soon thereafter at the edge of the Gulf of Severna, opposite the port of Sevastopol.

## The Fight in the Eastern Sector

As the battle dragged on, von Manstein realized that he had made a mistake: rather than attempting to break through the north, which was so heavily and fiercely defended by the forts, he should have sought to break through east of the entrenched camp. Though the terrain was much more mountainous there, the defenses were significantly less fearsome. Around June 17, he wanted to change tactics, but Halder decided that this maneuver would take too long, and Richthofen's air corps was about to be withdrawn in anticipation of von

This old T-26 has been literally shattered by an internal explosion, revealing the interior layout of the tank, with the driver's seat to the left and the imposing gearbox to the right. (Bundesarchiv)

Bock's offensive against the Caucasus and Stalingrad, which would begin on June 28. This explains why the efforts against the Sevastopol forts was renewed with vigor between June 17 and 19.

The battle in the eastern sector was also terrible, though not quite as furious in nature. The German objective there was to conquer, one by one, the rocky bastions where the Russians were entrenched: the North Nose, Chapel Mount, Tadpole Hill, Rose Hill, amongst the vineyards. A terrible melee had taken place in the British cemetery on the outskirts of the town in 1854–55.

Around June 25, the Russians still held Sevastopol, but the first two lines of defenses had been destroyed and the situation was very serious. Their calls for help could be answered only at night, when the Black Sea Fleet could operate without attracting the attentions of the Luftwaffe. Submarines brought around 4,000 tonnes of supplies and during the night of June 26, a new naval effort secured the landing of the 142nd Infantry Brigade.

Two German infantrymen crossing a Russian trench on the front at Sevastopol. The man on the left is carrying an MG 34 machine gun, while the man on the right is carrying an MP 38 or 40, better known (incorrectly) to the Allies as the Schmeisser, after an engineer from Haenel who developed certain armaments but was completely unrelated to this one. (Bundesarchiv)

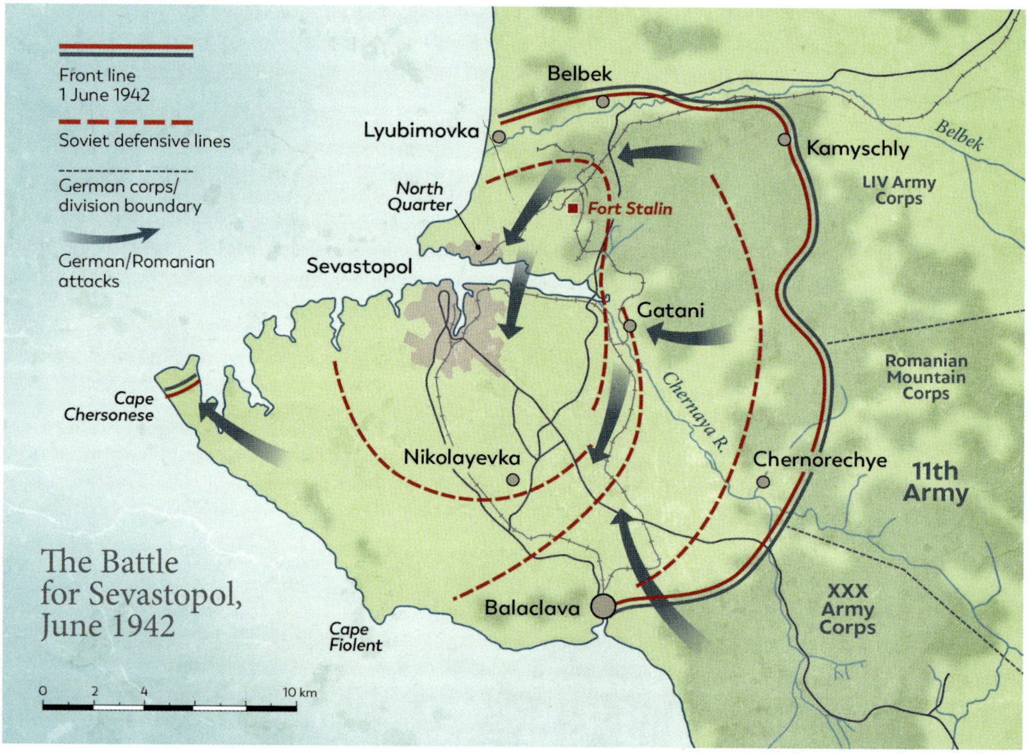

British aid launched into action at the beginning of 1942 to help the Red Army to replenish its equipment after their disastrous 1941; here, two damaged Hawker Hurricanes left behind on railroad flat car.

The Italians were also engaged in the Crimean Peninsula. This shot shows the stunning resources of the Fiat SPA 37 TL light artillery tractor, capable of pulling huge trailers. (Bundesarchiv)

## The Fall of Sevastopol

During the night of June 28, the assault troops of the 22nd and 24th Infantry Divisions crossed the Severna Bay in inflatable dinghies and landed behind the Russian defenses. This was the catalyst for the collapse of the Soviets in Sevastopol; from that point the battle was lost for the Russians, who fought tooth and nail to the bitter end.

Many defenders blew themselves up in their shelters or in their mountain hideouts. Von Manstein forbade his men from entering the city until it had been razed by artillery and aircraft fire. The surviving Russians tried to flee to the Korsun Peninsula, where they apparently hoped to be picked up by the Black Sea Fleet, but the sailors could not approach due to the Luftwaffe's attacks. On July 4, 30,000 men surrendered and the resistance in the Crimea was over. In total, the Germans took 90,000 prisoners and captured 467 guns. Sevastopol's political and military leaders, notably Admiral Oktyabrsky and General Petrov, escaped, either by submarine or speedboat, depending on the source.

The Eleventh Army's losses were far from negligible, amounting to 24,000 men. Indeed, in a curious epilog to this difficult yet victorious campaign, the army itself would disappear. Von Manstein was rewarded by Hitler, promoted to the rank of marshal. The Führer was so happy with von Manstein, he believed he could crush Leningrad as he crushed Sevastopol. As a result, he abandoned his plan for the Eleventh Army to cross the Kerch strait to invade the Kuban. Instead, von Manstein and his men were to be transferred to the other extremity of the front—the north. Halder, the Heer's chief of staff, emphatically opposed this, making the (rather sensible) point that it would be impossible to attack the Caucasus and Leningrad at the same time, or they would end up suffering the same disappointments as they had the previous year. A compromise was eventually reached—XXXXII Army Corps would be left in the Crimea, but the Eleventh Army, reduced to two corps, totaling four divisions (XXX and LIV Army Corps), would be sent to Leningrad. The remaining divisions would be divided up to serve as reinforcements in Smolensk and Crete. This dissolution of the Eleventh Army was a grave error, especially as it was the only German formation with experience fighting alongside Romanian troops. Months later, outside Stalingrad, their presence would be sorely missed.

Another view of the Maxim Gorky fortress and three of its 305mm pieces; the one in the foreground has a broken barrel. The size of the shells is quite remarkable. (Bundesarchiv)

The German infantry became confident following the taking of Sevastopol. (Bundesarchiv)

As on every front on which the Wehrmacht were engaged, the 88mm was practically omnipresent in the Crimea. (Bundesarchiv)

# In Profile:
# Soviet Trucks and Armored Vehicles

An old Soviet truck from 1925–28, likely a Type Ya 3. Still very widespread in the Red Army in 1942, it weighed around 3 tonnes. The identification number displayed here has been extrapolated from the system used by Soviet forces. The driver entered by the open right-side of the vehicle; there was no door.

*Right:* The six-wheeled BA-10 was developed in 1938, and first saw action in Manchuria in 1938. It was the most produced Soviet heavy armored car in the first years of the war with over 3,000 built, in three variants, but was rarely seen after the winter of 1941/42. Its armor was up to 15mm thick at the front and on the turret. It had a 50 hp engine, and could be converted to a half-track by fitting auxiliary tracks to the rear wheels. The tracks were helpful when the vehicle was traversing soft ground or snow. It had a crew of four men and was armed with a 45mm gun and two machine guns. Large numbers of BA-10s were captured and used by the Germans.

*Above:* A copy of the famous Ford AA—the GAZ AA—widely used by both the Soviets and the Germans. Though archaic, it revealed itself, despite only having rear-wheel drive, to be excellent over difficult terrain. The role of these vehicles proved of paramount importance in the conduct of operations

*Left:* Rear detail of the GAZ AA. The identification number was also painted on the doors of the cab.

A column of new Panzer IIIs at the beginning of or on the eve of the German summer offensive. These are excellent examples of the PzKpfw III Ausf. J with long 50mm KwK L/60 main guns. The frontal armor was clearly considered insufficient by the crews, who have apparently reinforced it with spare track. On the mudguard, the insignia of the 23rd Panzer Division—a stylized Eiffel Tower—can just be made out. (Bundesarchiv)

# The German Plan

On April 5, 1942, Hitler issued his Directive no. 41, which outlined the upcoming Eastern offensive. In it he established the general aims of the new attack, namely to destroy Russia's military power by separating the Red Army from the sources of its armament. Suffice it to say, it didn't really go into the specifics of how this might be achieved. It implied that all enemy forces west of the Don had to be destroyed, after which the Germans could seize the oil fields of the Caucasus as well as

The small Panzer IIs coexisted alongside the Panzer IV Ausf. F2s armed with a formidable long 75mm gun. (Bundesarchiv)

Two tanks from 9th Panzer Division in spring 1942. The insignia on the Panzer II in the foreground is perfectly visible. Behind it, the Panzer IV is an Ausf. D or E, maybe F1, armed with a short 75mm gun. (Bundesarchiv)

the hills that would open the path towards Turkey and Iran. It did not mention Stalingrad, nor the Volga, and just as in the plan for *Barbarossa*, Moscow was not named as a target.

To ward off the threat of the Soviet heavy tanks, the Panzerjager units needed new materiel, and were provided with a powerful asset: the Marder II, equipped here with a Russian 76.2mm gun. Contrary to the appearance of its undercarriage, it was actually built on the chassis of a Panzer II. This was a creation of the Alkett company. (Bundesarchiv)

A Heer truck crosses a bridge recently built by German engineers. The silhouette of the vehicle is familiar: it's clearly a Renault. (Bundesarchiv)

## Important Economic Considerations

The conquest of the Caucasus mountains was key to a grandiose strategy to create a link in the Middle East between the German troops—coming from the Kuban—and Rommel's Afrikakorps, then to the gates of Alexandria. It's not totally clear whether Hitler actually thought such a maneuver would be possible, but the fact of the matter was that he didn't have the numbers to open up a new front that was not related to the destruction of the Soviet Union.

The oil wells in the Caucasus were a different matter, as they were absolutely essential to the Russian war effort. In 1940, the total oil production was 31 million tonnes and in 1941, it reached 38 million tonnes. A sizeable proportion of this oil came from three large fields: Maykop, Grozny, and Baku. According to Western experts at the time, 80% of production came from Baku (71.5% according to Soviet sources). These were not the only oil fields in the USSR; oil fields could also be found in the Urals, on the upper Volga and to the east of the Caspian Sea, however these areas were fully developed, but produced only 14% of the Soviet total oil output in 1941: the Caucasus was crucial.

Hitler's Directive no. 41, issued in April 1942, called for a consolidation of the entire Eastern Front in preparation for breakthrough into the Caucasus, followed by capture of Leningrad in the north. His aim was to devastate Soviet forces in the south but more importantly capture economic resources that would facilitate the German war effort. His generals, however, continued to prioritize the destruction of the Soviet army.

The oil was channeled towards the center of Russia by diverse routes. Pipelines led from Baku and Grozny to the Black Sea, but these were few and of limited capacity. Moreover, an important part of the Black Sea was now in German hands. Transport by barge along the Volga was more common, with around 9 million tonnes making the journey by boat each year.

Railway transportation was by far the most important method of transportation for oil, with a total capacity of 29 million tonnes per year. By cutting off the railroads connecting the Caucasus to Russia, the Germans could asphyxiate the Red Army and Soviet aviation, which in summer 1941 consumed 4.5 million tonnes of fuel.

## The Plan of Attack

The German plan of attack consisted of three offensives launched one after the other, along a west–east axis, the armies placed to the north attacking first. The first of these attacks, combining the attacking power of 9th Panzer Division, the 3rd Motorized Infantry Division, the Grossdeutschland Division, the 16th Motorized Infantry Division, and 24th Panzer Division (not to mention the infantry divisions that followed), was directed against Voronezh and aimed at the Don. Next, the motorized and armored elements of this army would turn towards the southeast, along the Don, to drive the enemy back towards the south, at the same time triggering the attack from Kharkov. This was evidently to surround the Soviet troops to the west of the Don. These elements would be the 100th Mountain Division, the 23rd Panzer Division, the 29th Motorized Infantry Division, the 336th Infantry Division, and the 3rd Panzer Division. Finally, the third parallel push, directed towards Stalingrad, would surround the city, all units thrusting from the north. It was no longer about taking Stalingrad, but Hitler insisted that it should be submitted to artillery fire so that it could no longer serve the Soviet war effort economically. Halder and von Bock, little inclined to fight in the streets, opposed the idea that the city should be a priority. Indeed, the railroad from Astrakhan on the coast of the Caspian Sea to the interior of the country veered off to the north before it reached Stalingrad, leaving only one way into the city. The Germans would have to cut the railroad south of Stalingrad.

However, Hitler insisted more and more that Stalingrad be considered a primary objective, probably because of the symbolic weight that capturing it would carry.

A wonderful example of a Sturmgeschütz 40 Ausf. F belonging to the elite Grossdeutschland division. (Bundesarchiv)

# In Profile: Soviet Aircraft

Conceived by the Soviets as an assault plane, the Ilyushin Il-2 became one of the most formidable planes of World War II. According to German pilots, it was the most difficult plane to shoot down. Its 730 kg of armor effectively made it a flying tank (albeit very slowly and close to the ground). The Il-2 was a difficult target for German fighters, as it absorbed even the heaviest blows. A fair number of novice pilots in the Reich were shot down by its rear 12.7mm machine gun. The 20mm wing-mounted cannons and, later, rockets, constituted a colossal strike force for the time. Many enemy tanks fell victim to the Il-2.

The LaGG-3 represents one of the Soviet Union's first steps towards aerial supremacy. Of modern conception, and endowed with "serious" firepower (23mm gun, two 20mm machine guns or guns), it was a tough opponent. With the arrival of the LaGG-5 and LaGG-7, the Russians had at their disposal planes superior to the Bf 109s, especially at low altitude. Some German pilots crashed into the ground trying to follow them. Their low-altitude acrobatics required enormous skill on the part of the Russian pilots; German pilots never came close to having enough maneuverability.

The appearance of the Yak 3 tolled the death knell for German aerial superiority on the Russian Front. This plane preceded the Yak 9 which would become, according to certain aviation historians, the greatest fighter of the war. Already, the Yaks 1 and 3 were superior to the Bf 109 Fs when under 6,000 m on all fronts. Around 8,700 Yak 1s and 4,900 Yak 3s were built during World War II.

This postcard depicting the Square of the Fallen Fighters, Stalingrad, c. 1941 is in stark contrast to the famous photographs of the ruins of the city after the battle.

## In Profile: Stalingrad

Stalingrad was symbolically important not only because it bore the name of Stalin, but also because it was a symbol of the civil war between the Bolsheviks and the White Russians in 1918, when all the latter's assaults against the city, then called Tsaritsyn, were repelled by Stalin, Vorochilov, and Budyonny.

The city became a center of heavy industry under Stalin and by the time of Operation *Barbarossa* was home to over 400,000 people.

A Panzer II of the general staff of 2nd Battalion, 201st Panzer Regiment, 23rd Panzer Division. This unit was created in October 1941, in the Paris area before joining the Eastern Front in June 1942. It retained the divisional insignia adopted during its stay in France—the Eiffel Tower—on all its vehicles, including this Panzer II, but also the SdKfz 251s in the photo opposite. The gun seen on the Panzer II is a fake, to leave more room inside the turret. (Bundesarchiv)

An impressive column of 23rd Panzer Division's materiel. The newly created panzer division was given first-rate vehicles that were often filmed or photographed by the propaganda units. The division's panzergrenadier regiments were numbered 126th and 128th. (Bundesarchiv)

## Army Group South

Von Bock's offensive involved only Army Group South, the rest of the front remaining on the defensive. The forces on the front, Army Groups Center and North, comprised an impressive 96 divisions, though most of them were not at full strength. The offensive, whose objectives were spread over more than 2,000 km, could only be launched by a relatively limited number of divisions. On June 16, 1942, Halder recorded the following distribution of men across the Heer:

Eastern Front:

- Army Group North: 36 divisions
- Army Group Center: 63 divisions
- Army Group South: 68 divisions

Other fronts:

- Finland: 5 divisions
- Norway: 12 divisions
- France: 26 divisions
- The Balkans: 5 divisions
- Germany: 3 divisions
- Africa: 3 divisions

The Italian army sent six infantry divisions to serve within Army Group South. Shown in this photo is a Fiat Spa TL 37 light artillery tractor; note the small Italian pennant displaying the Savoie family crest. (Bundesarchiv)

This amounts to a total of 167 divisions on the Eastern Front and 54 across the other fronts. The fear of an invasion from Norway incited Hitler to keep at least 12 divisions there, yet the other most important front, the North African theater, was only held by three divisions.

The problem of manpower was crucial on the Eastern Front at the beginning of summer in 1942, especially since the threat of the Allies soon forced more formations to leave for the West. In July, Army Group South only comprised 52 German divisions instead of 68; on July 1, the German armies consisted of 2,847,000 men on the Eastern Front and 971,000 men in all other theaters. Just one year earlier, there had been 3,206,000 men in Russia and 594,000 men in other theaters. To address this 400,000-man deficit, the Heer had to call on its allies, the Hungarian, Romanian and Italian armies. Direct pressure from Hitler allowed the Heer to line up 28 new, non-German divisions to support Army Group South: 12 divisions of the Romanian army; 10 divisions of the Hungarian army; and six divisions of the Italian army. The smaller contribution by Italy was due to the fact that Italy was also fighting on two fronts, and sending large battalions to support the Panzerarmee Afrika.

A Junkers Ju 86E-2 from the Hungarian "air army," shot down in south Russia. This model was no longer in service in the Luftwaffe at this time.

An excellent view of a Panzer III Ausf. J of the 24th Panzer Division. This unit was an old cavalry division, as their insignia shows. It was remodeled into a panzer division in East Prussia during November 1941. Its panzer regiment was numbered 24th. (Bundesarchiv)

The issue of the Romanians and Hungarians was delicate, to say the least, for the Germans. Since Romania had been forced to cede important territory to Hungary, antagonism between the two peoples was virulent and there was no question of Hungarians and Romanians fighting side by side. In addition, due to national pride, the Italians and Hungarians categorically refused to fight under German control or with German reinforcements. The OKH, aware of the relative weakness of these units, which represented at the time approximately one-third of Army Group South, entrusted them with only a defensive mission on the northeastern front, on the banks of the Don, once they reached it.

An interesting shot of a rarely photographed aircraft: a Heinkel He 46C, a reconnaissance craft re-purposed in Russia for night-harassment operations. (Bundesarchiv)

On July 4, 1942, the composition of Army Group South was as follows:

| Army | Panzer Division | Motorized Infantry Division | Infantry Division | Hungarian | Romanian | Italian |
|---|---|---|---|---|---|---|
| Second Army | 0 | 1 | 4 | 2 | 0 | 0 |
| Fourth Panzer Army | 3 | 1 | 6 | 0 | 0 | 0 |
| 2nd Hungarian Army | 0 | 0 | 0 | 4 | 0 | 0 |
| Sixth Army | 2 | 1 | 15 | 0 | 0 | 0 |
| First Panzer Army | 3 | 1 | 7 | 0 | 4 | 0 |
| Seventeenth Army | 1 | 1 | 6 | 0 | 4 | 6 |

The allies' divisions were not yet all in place. Von Bock had nine panzer divisions, around the same number as there were at the invasion of France, but less than half the number amassed for Operation *Barbarossa*. Theoretically, the panzer divisions of 1942 were the same strength as those of 1941, and the equipment was about the same: Panthers and Tigers were still at an experimental stage in Germany, but the Panzer IIIs and IVs had seen some upgrades, mostly in relation to firepower.

As such, the Panzer IIIs were at the time armed with 50mm L/60 main guns with high initial velocity (Ausf. J, L, and M), while the Panzer IV Ausf. F2s, armed with long 75mm main guns, also made an appearance. The Panzer 38 (t) and Panzer II (Ausf. F) were still present too, and even the Panzer I had not totally disappeared, even though their use was only anecdotal.

From an aerial point of view, von Richthofen's Air Fleet 4 had at its disposal 10 *Jagdgeschwader* (Messerschmitt Bf 109 and FW 190); 8 *Zerstörergeschwader* (twin-engined Messerschmitt Bf 110); 16 *Kampfgeschwader* (Do 17, He 111, and Ju 88); and 5 *Stukageschwader* (Ju 87).

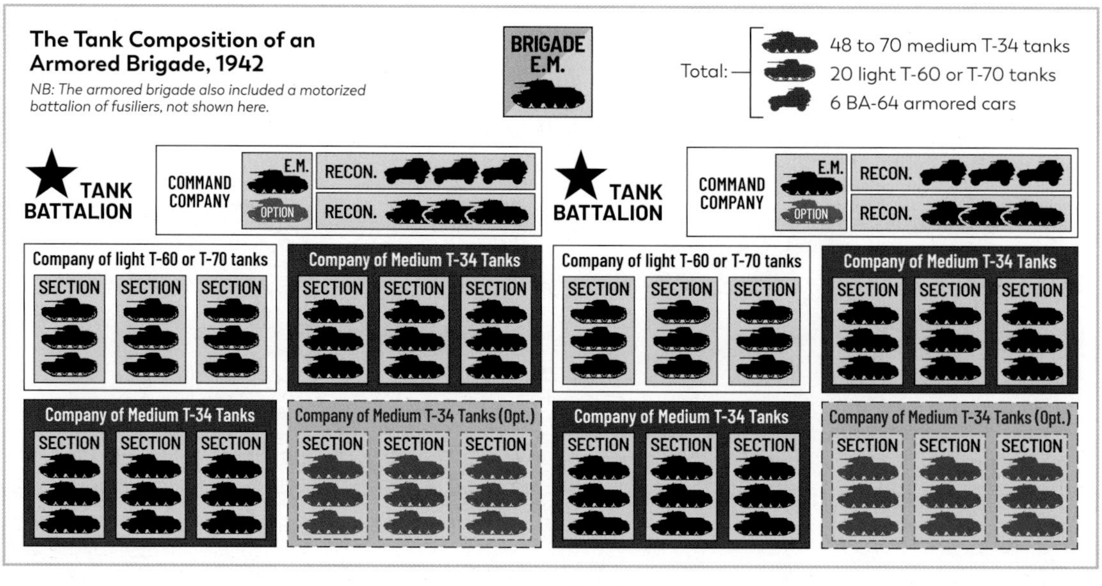

# The Reorganization of the Armored Soviet Army in 1942

The battle of Moscow was not a tank victory, even though 20 armored brigades and around the same number of battalions were deployed in December 1941 during the Zhukov counteroffensive. The weather meant that the infantry assumed the leading role. Still, in some cases, the involvement of tanks was a determining factor, notably when armored units were launched in advance to capture vital objectives, such as road junctions or dominant positions. The Red Army suffered so much in the first months of the campaign that no thorough reorganization was possible and the units intervening in the battle had little cohesion.

On January 22, 1942, the Soviet high command made important arrangements that laid the groundwork for future Soviet armored warfare doctrine. In particular, it was decided that "for the success of a fast and deep offensive, it is necessary to use, as well as armored units to support the infantry, large armored formations that are autonomous and carry out independent operations." This clearly required a very considerable number of tanks, which Russian industry was fortunately capable of producing—in 1942, Soviet tank production reached an enormous 24,668 units. However this barely allowed them to make up for the losses at the front, and in May 1942, the Red Army owned 4,659 tanks and in November, 6,596. This would imply that nearly 15,000 tanks were lost during 1942.

This massive introduction of tanks allowed a complete restructuring of armored forces in spring 1942. This didn't just concern the make-up of individual units, but also their tactical use. Thus, it was decided that the autonomous armored brigades and battalions would not be launched into battle alone, but with the support of artillery and aviation and, perhaps most importantly, only on terrain that had been sufficiently reconnoitered in advance.

Two main types of armored units were created, which mirrored the composition of pre-war units, but with a lot more flexibility.

The armored corps had three armored brigades (see diagram opposite) and an infantry brigade, for a total of 168 tanks.

Paradoxically, the mechanized corps had more tanks—175 in total—divided between three mechanized brigades and one armored brigade.

The diagram opposite shows an important formation, which fluctuated a lot in its composition: the armored army, of which the first two (3rd and 5th) appeared in April/May 1942. They were composed of armored corps, infantry divisions, cavalry units, and artillery.

These new formations went into battle for the first time in spring 1942, at Kharkov, then on the fronts at Voronezh and Bryansk, and finally in the fights preceding the battle of Stalingrad.

This Valentine infantry tank has just been delivered to the Red Army. Its armor would have satisfied the Soviets, but they would have been disappointed in its 2-pdr (40mm) gun, which was very poor compared to the 76.2mm guns of the KV-1 and T-34. (Bundesarchiv)

## The Red Army

After the disastrous battle of Kharkov, the Southwestern Front was no more than a shadow of its former self. The table on page 60 shows the theoretical composition of the Soviet units, but in reality, particularly during the first weeks of the German offensive, it was undoubtedly different, though no source can provide precise details. Therefore the numbers quoted should be taken as estimates rather than exact data.

This farm tractor has been armored by the Russians and armed with a 45mm gun. It was a makeshift vehicle little suited to combat. (Bundesarchiv)

Go east! A Panzer IV Ausf. F2 crosses a German trench as it advances towards the enemy. It doesn't bear a divisionary insignia, but it does have a tactical symbol from the panzer regiment, which appears to have been painted over. (Bundesarchiv)

# Case *Blau*

## The first of three German pushes towards the East began on June 28, 1942, with 17 German divisions—three of which were armored divisions—and six Hungarian divisions.

The Germans didn't gain any advantage from the element of surprise, as on June 19, the operations officer of the 23rd Panzer Division, Major Reichel, crashed behind Soviet lines in his Fieseler Storch, carrying in his pannier the maps for Case *Blau*. When General Georg Stumme, commander of XXXX Panzer Corps, found out, he dispatched a battalion to find him. The little plane was found, but Reichel, the pilot, and the pannier were gone. A little later, two graves were found and excavated. The two corpses had been stripped of their uniforms, so Reichel's aide-de-camp was brought in to identify his boss's body. While the Russians had not been able to interrogate Reichel, his pannier and the maps therein had been recovered by the Soviets. After studying them, the Stavka deduced that the first objective of Case *Blau I* was the capture of Voronezh. What would happen after that was uncertain, as it appeared Reichel wasn't carrying maps for later operations. For the Soviets, the capture of Voronezh was without doubt the first step in a vast operation that would turn to Moscow from the south. Measures were immediately taken to reinforce the troops in the northern Don sector, which effectively took troops away from the southern—and most immediately threatened—sector of the front.

It was in a Fieseler Storch like this that Major Reichel—and the plans for Case *Blau*—crashed behind Russian lines. (Bundesarchiv)

On the German side, the "Reichel incident" had not gone unnoticed. It was too late for a change of plans, but those in charge—General Stumme and General von Boineburg, commander of the 23rd Panzer Division—were subjected to a court-martial presided over by Goering, relieved of command and sentenced to imprisonment. The sentence, however, was quickly commuted and Stumme was sent to northern Africa to take command of the Afrikakorps. He was killed at the beginning of the battle of El Alamein.

## The Russians Reorganize

After the defeat at Kharkov, Timoshenko lost command of the Southwestern Front and was left in charge of only the Northwestern Front. The Stavka took direct command of the other two fronts in the sector, the Southern and the Bryansk. Finally, after the loss of the Crimea, a North Caucasian Front was established, with Budyonny at its head.

A column comprising three Panzer IIIs and a Panzer II moves past a Russian village not far from the Don. At the rear is one of 23rd Panzer Division's "Eiffel Tower" tanks. (Bundesarchiv)

A line of T-34s in perfect condition surprised by the Germans at the beginning of their advance. This view shows how the tanks were secured onto the transport by a strap hooked to a loop between the two exhaust pipes. (Bundesarchiv)

The discovery of the German maps only reinforced the Soviet high command's opinion that the next offensive would be brought against Moscow.

This error was principally due to German propaganda, which since February had increasingly mentioned an attack on Moscow. Also, following and understanding Hitler's intentions from day to day was not an easy job for his own generals, so for the Stavka it was an almost impossible task.

In the days preceding the German attack, the Bryansk Front was reinforced with four armored corps, four armored brigades, and the equivalent of six infantry divisions. But these troops were surprised by the enemy assault before they reached their designated positions.

A traffic jam at a bridge over an anonymous river, somewhere south of Voronezh. The vehicles photographed once again come from 23rd Panzer Division. The side-car in the foreground is interesting as it has two divisionary insignias on its mudguard: the usual Eiffel Tower and an arrow crossed by a perpendicular line towards its base. (Bundesarchiv)

These artillerymen are taking a break as they wait to recommence firing on the Soviet positions. The photo is intriguing: the men are not posing for the camera and seem tired, or lost in their thoughts. They are wearing earplugs. The gun is an s.F.H. 18 (150mm), as can be seen from the box of shells. (Bundesarchiv)

This rider from a motorcycle unit (whose tactical insignia we can see on the mudguard, under the license plate) comes from 24th Panzer Division, previously the 1st Cavalry Division from East Prussia. The divisionary insignia is clearly visible. The panzer-gray paint job has been covered with a paler color, probably sand, and only the insignias stand out against this background. The side-car is a 750cc s Kraftrad BMW R75 mit Seltenwagen. (Bundesarchiv)

Two vehicles modified to transport artillery pieces. On the right is an SdKfz 251/10 with a 3.7cm Pak 35/36, and on the left is an SdKfz 6 carrying a 37mm anti-aircraft gun. (Bundesarchiv)

## The Germans Crush the Front

On June 28 at 0215 hrs, Hoth's Fourth Panzer Army rushed forward, led by 24th Panzer Division, supported to the north by the Grossdeutschland Motorized Division and to the south by the 16th Motorized Infantry Division. On Hoth's left flank was the Second Army and to the right the 2nd Hungarian Army.

The 24th Panzer Division, formerly the 1st Cavalry Division of East Prussia, attacked without considering its neighboring units. It struck between the 13th and 40th Soviet Armies and repelled them, quickly creating a breach which they then enlarged. To face this, General Fedorenko counterattacked on June 30 with three armored corps, but the Russians were not able to gain the upper hand over their adversaries, who were tactically superior and had mastered attacking in combination with aviation. In addition, Fedorenko sent his tanks into battle as soon as they arrived at the front, without regrouping them first. This division of forces led rapidly to disaster, and the KV-1s and other T-34s, despite being superior to the panzers, were beaten, destroyed, and dispersed.

A Sturmgeschütz 40 Ausf F charges at full speed through a Russian village. The unit insignia on its flank is unfortunately obscured. (Bundesarchiv)

This Sturmgeschütz III Ausf.E has just destroyed a KV-1 (burning in the background). There is a good, clear insignia of a knight on its armor plating.

# From the Eiffel Tower to the Don

On June 30, 1942, Sixth Army joined the offensive, leaving the Volchansk region for Voronezh, supported by IV Air Corps. The XXXX Panzer Corps was destined to advance towards the Don and form a pincer to join the troops of the Fourth Panzer Army and create a large encirclement in the style of Operation *Barbarossa*. With 100th Mountain Division, 29th Motorized Infantry Division, 3rd Panzer Division, and 23rd Panzer Division, XXXX Panzer Corps was strong and stable. Only the 23rd Panzer Division, new on the front, had not experienced enemy fire. Its divisional emblem at the time was a stylized Eiffel Tower, referring to its previous assignment in France. When the Soviets learned of their presence on the front, they welcomed the division by dropping leaflets on them, which read as follows:

> **Soldiers of 23rd Panzer Division, the Soviet Union salutes you! Your gay days in Paris are over now. Your comrades will already have warned you about what is happening here. Soon you will find out for yourselves.**

A fire has ravaged this KV-1. The Russians were incapable of responding to the German offensive and were forced into a speedy retreat, which surprised not only the Germans but also the Stavka, who continued to call for a halt to the withdrawal. (Bundesarchiv)

The materiel used by both sides during the summer of 1942 was not always the most up to date. Take as an example this German horse-drawn carriage, which is driving past the remains of a light T-60 tank, the equivalent of a German Panzer II. (Bundesarchiv)

In fact during the first days of the campaign, the men of 23rd Panzer Division did not experience anything like the hell described by survivors of the battle of Moscow. On the contrary, the Russian resistance was nothing extraordinary: apart from a solid rearguard that fought with determination, the Soviet troops avoided combat and retreated eastwards. Was this a new Soviet tactic? The commander of XXXX Panzer Corps wanted to follow them to the east, rather than effect the pincer movement around Voronezh, as he doubted the pincer would "grab" anything worthwhile. But Paulus told him that he had to follow orders, and link up with the elements of the Fourth Panzer Army marching on Voronezh as quickly as possible.

This small armored vehicle rolling through the streets of Voronezh is not of German origin: it is a Russian T-60 with its turret removed. An MG 34 has nonetheless been installed by its German crew. (Bundesarchiv)

In Voronezh or Rostov, a Panzer III Ausf L or M that has added frontal armor, but which has lost the additional plating from around its main gun. It has a regimental insignia on the flank of its turret. (Bundesarchiv)

A Panzer II of 24th Panzer Division crosses a stream on a rickety bridge. A large SdKfz 7 has been abandoned after getting bogged down fording the stream. (Bundesarchiv)

This is a typical combination for German motorized artillery units: an m Zgkw 5-tonne Typ BN L 9, SdKfz 6/1, with a 10.5cm FH 18 howitzer. (Bundesarchiv)

This link-up was achieved on July 2, and parts of the 21st and 40th Soviet Armies were captured. The prisoner headcount was easily done, as there were only 20,000–30,000 men in the pocket, an especially disappointing number given almost all of their heavy materiel had escaped capture. The first phase of Case *Blau* therefore ended up being a waste of time.

## The Voronezh Question

On July 3, 1942, while the German troops were rapidly approaching Voronezh, facing an increasingly elusive enemy, Hitler went to von Bock's command post to discuss the situation. In light of the Russian retreat, it now seemed useless to seize Voronezh, which would take time—time that could not be lost if they wanted to pursue their adversaries. As a result of the consultation, Hitler authorized von Bock to put Voronezh (which is east of the Don and served by a river that could act as a rampart against eventual counterattack) on the proverbial back burner. This was good reasoning, but for some unknown reason, Hitler was pusillanimous, leaving the decision to von Bock rather than making the decision himself.

Von Bock was irritated at having to make the call himself. Capturing Voronezh would create a strong defensive point on the left flank. However, significant forces would be needed to take the town. Rather than making a firm decision, von Bock chose to wait to see what opportunity might arise to facilitate one route or the other. This indecision at the highest level was typical of the German army during the two world wars—seen at the battle of Marne in 1914, at Dunkirk in May 1940, and in Russia during autumn 1941. It is surprising, then, that in the field the Germans showed a spirit of communal decisiveness largely superior to that of the Russians and even the British.

These four photographs show the different phases of the reduction of a village or group of huts by German infantry supported by an artillery piece—in this first image, a 50mm anti-tank gun, a gun arguably unsuited to this task. This may indicate that these images have been put together for use in propaganda. Still, they are impressive. Below and opposite, two different guns open fire on a relatively close target—a group of huts a few hundred meters from the village. The infantrymen are on their bellies, ready to advance. (Bundesarchiv)

Russian soldiers leave a smoking barn, towards which German soldiers are marching. Then the Russian prisoners pass by the side of a Pak gun; the gunners are keeping an eye on the horizon, as if looking out for the enemy. (Bundesarchiv)

Though once a feared adversary of the Germans, the Matilda II no longer seemed as great a threat following the failure of Operation *Battleaxe* in Cyrenaica. This model shows a modification added by the Russians; shaped sheet-metal guards around the headlights to block peripheral light from dazzling or distracting the driver. (Bundesarchiv)

On July 4 at 2000 hrs, a *kampfgruppe* from the Grossdeutschland Division seized a bridge over the Don, moments before it was blown up. The men, supported by Sturmgeschütz IIIs, then took advantage of the opportunity to attempt a reconnaissance mission into the heart of Voronezh. They reached the train station, but were forced to retreat when they met the Soviet garrison.

Faced with the proximity of Voronezh, von Bock decided to jump on the town as quickly as possible, making use of the element of surprise. Several units, notably the Grossdeutschland and the 24th Panzer Division, amassed at the bridgeheads to the east of the Don, ready to attack. But on July 5, Hitler gave von Bock firm orders to halt the attack and head south.

Another view of the bridge over the Don tributary. A quad-mounted 20mm Flak gun, mounted on an SPW, is camouflaged in the rushes. Russian aviation was active mostly in the early hours of the morning before the German aircraft appeared. (Bundesarchiv)

This Bücher 181, camouflaged with foliage, is waiting for a new propeller. This small aircraft was used in Russia as a liaison craft. (Bundesarchiv)

The next morning, elements of the Grossdeutschland and the 24th Panzer Division announced that they had reached the center of Voronezh. Von Bock immediately warned Hitler, who reconsidered his decision of the previous day and agreed to the capture of the town, on the condition that no element of Sixth Army participated and that the armored divisions of the Fourth Panzer Army continued their movements southwards.

Though the taking of Voronezh was announced on German radio on July 7, the battle raged for over a week, as the Germans lacked the troops to ensure a decisive victory. The units marching towards the south were also struggling, albeit for a different reason: they had run out of gas. These delays would have grave consequences for von Bock.

## Change of Command and Tactics

*Blau III* began on July 7, with General Ruoff's Seventeenth Army and von Kleist's First Panzer Army taking the lead. The south wing was placed under the command of a new army group, Army Group A, commanded by Wilhelm List, which officially became operational on July 9. The First Panzer Army made swift progress; the Russians had no intention of becoming trapped, and the fronts to the south and southwest were withdrawing quickly eastwards, crossing the Don at a suitable crossing. Further south, however, progress towards Rostov was slow and difficult.

A general overview of the battle is necessary here, as it developed in a very confusing way. To the north, the Fourth Panzer Army was still near Voronezh on July 9; the town had still not been completely conquered. The lack of fuel disrupted maneuvers further south, where Paulus's Sixth Army had been marching along the Don towards Stalingrad, relatively unhindered by Russian resistance. Further south still, the First Panzer Army was advancing between the Donets and the Don with disconcerting ease. Finally, in the extreme south, violent fighting was raging around Rostov and in the industrial basins nearby.

Even in this low-angle shot, the Panzer II looks unimpressive in 1942, especially when the tank commander is standing in the turret (Bundesarchiv)

In short, the German center was not experiencing any major problems, but its two wings were struggling to make any progress. This worried an already troubled von Bock, who was becoming obsessed with the threat facing the Germans from north of Voronezh and along the Don. The soldiers on the front were themselves worried, as can be gleaned from a report in *Völkischer Beobachter*, the Nazi Party's newspaper:

> **The Russians, who up to this time had fought stubbornly over each kilometer, withdrew without firing a shot. Our advance was only delayed by destroyed bridges and by aircraft. When the Soviet rearguards were too hard-pressed, they chose a position which enabled them to hold out until night ... It was quite disquieting to plunge into this vast area without finding a trace of the enemy.**[1]

In an attempt to finally seize the enemy, Hitler intervened directly in the course of the battle on July 9, and ordered Hoth to abandon the Voronezh sector, and go south to rendezvous with Kleist's tanks near Millerovo, forming a vast crucible.

By the time the two panzer armies met at Millerovo, most of the Soviets had already escaped, and only 14,000 men were captured by the Germans. Since the beginning of the offensive, Army Group South—divided in two, Army Groups A and B, since July 9—had taken fewer than 50,000 prisoners. So where was the enemy? Aerial recon missions hadn't discovered anything between the Donets and the Don. Hitler was convinced that rather than retreating to the east, towards the Volga and Stalingrad, the Russians had retreated southwards, into the loop of the Don, which would explain the difficulties experienced by the German troops at Rostov.

As a result, Hitler ordered Hoth's Fourth Panzer Army to make a U-turn, and instead of advancing southeast, to go southwest, to finally begin the great encirclement battle that he had been waiting for.

The maneuver was ordered without consulting von Bock, who lost no time in complaining about it to the OKH. Since Army Group South had been split into two and he no longer commanded Army Group B, he faced off against the OKH several times. On July 13, Keitel telephoned him to tell him that the Führer had decided to hand Army Group B over to General von Weichs, and that as a result, it would be good if von Bock resigned for "health reasons" to save face. When von Bock asked why he was being dismissed, Keitel told him that Hitler held him responsible for the fuel shortages during the second week of the offensive. Left with little alternative, von Bock resigned, and did not hold another command

1 Clark, Alan. *Barbarossa: The Russian German Conflict 1941–1945*. London: Weidenfeld & Nicolson, 1995.

position for the rest of the war. Von Weichs took command of Army Group B and List remained head of Army Group A.

On the ground, there was considerable confusion, as all the armored elements had been diverted to Rostov. Paulus alone continued moving towards Stalingrad, without even XXXX Panzer Corps. The panzers were taking them in the opposite direction, but not without trouble, as sudden storms disrupted their progress, and elsewhere delayed the distribution of fuel. Suddenly, on July 18, Hitler changed his mind: it was clear that the Russians had left the loop of the Don and had retreated towards the Caucasus, leaving only Rostov defended while the bulk of the force fled. Consequently, the panzer divisions turned back around towards the east, XXXX Panzer Corps returning to Sixth Army while the Fourth and First Panzer Armies crossed the lower Don as they made their way towards the Volga.

After three weeks of battle, almost everything between the Don and the Donets had been conquered. But the Red Army had lost fewer than 80,000 prisoners, which was very little in proportion to Russia's immense reserves. The first phase of the offensive therefore had a mixed result: a large advance in the south of Russia, at relatively small cost, but with the ultimate goal of the destruction of the Red Army not yet even hinted at. Certainly at the time, Hitler and the OKH were not completely appraised of the true situation; on July 15, the following conversation took place in the Führer's HQ:

> **Hitler: "The Russians are finished!"**
> **Halder: "Well they're certainly giving us that impression."**

Indeed, Timoshenko's armies, decimated at Kharkov in May, had not recovered from the disaster and, totally incapable of opposing the German offensive at the end of June, had no other alternative but to retreat as quickly as possible. Yet it was not von Bock's offensive that had depleted Timoshenko's troops, and the Russian reserves elsewhere were being replenished. The three *Blau* operations had only really succeeded in clearing up the units that had either already been destroyed or were too badly damaged to recover. The Red Army was not finished, and the first phase of the battle had not allowed the Germans to bring home a decisive victory. They were, however, in an excellent position for advancing on the one hand towards the oil wells of the Caucasus, and on the other towards the Volga and Stalingrad.

GAZ trucks seemed to have a worrying tendency to lose parts of their engine cowlings. This particular example, however, can claim mitigating circumstances. (Bundesarchiv)

# In Profile:
# Medium and Heavy Soviet Tanks

The first production T-34s were completed in September 1940, but only around 400 were built before production switched to the Model 1941, which had heavier armor, and a superior main gun, the F-34. Both the T-34 and the KV tanks surprised the Germans when they encountered them in battle. The KV-1 tanks had thicker armor protection than the T-34, and initially the only German weapon able to take it on was the 88mm Flak gun.

A T-34 from 1941/42 encountered by 1st Battalion, 13th Panzer Division. The engine appears to have been built in the Barrikady factory and sent immediately to the front. The life expectancy of a T-34 was so short that the tanks often went into combat before they were even painted.

A T-34 Model 1941. Despite the widespread use of these tanks, the German advance was not halted or even slowed down. The price paid by the Soviets was a terrible one, but the German army showed signs of fatigue, and supplies were no longer arriving; German production was no longer meeting the increasingly important demand for materials.

A KV-1A encountered in the Bykow sector. The patriotic slogans painted on this tank spread throughout the Soviet ranks following the German defeat outside Moscow. These inscriptions were yellow, white, red, or black.

The Sturmgeschütz 40s were frequently photographed during the summer of 1942, as their low profile and long 75mm gun are impressive. They symbolized the power regained by the Wehrmacht after the terrible winter of 1941–42. (Bundesarchiv)

The Soviets tried to block this road with scavenged items, including the fuselage of a Stormvik, attacked on the ground. This photo appears to have been taken in Rostov or its environs. (Bundesarchiv)

# | Towards the Caucasus

The Soviet front had exploded over more than 300 km in width, but to the south, the withdrawal was going well.

The pillar of the Russian defense was the town of Rostov-on-Don. On July 19, General Ruoff's Seventeenth Army managed to break the opposing front and his LVII Panzer Corps were immediately launched forwards. This was composed of 13th Panzer Division, the SS-Wiking Motorized Division, the 125th Infantry Division, and the Slovak Fast Division. These units formed one arm of a pincer, moving in from the west; the other arm, attacking from the north, consisted of the 14th and 22nd Panzer Divisions of III Panzer Corps.

The fighting was particularly ferocious in the west, where the SS and the 13th Panzer Division reached the outer edges of the town. Getting into Rostov was a challenge, as the Russians had decided to

A very Caucasian scene—water is being brought to the troops by camel. Water was the most sorely needed supply for the motorized German units—the Caucasus mountains themselves are preceded by seemingly endless desert steppes. (Bundesarchiv)

Another shot of a large town—again, maybe Rostov—destroyed by the bitter fighting. A German war trophy rolls through the square: a Soviet gun and its tractor, a stripped-down light T-70 tank. (Bundesarchiv)

ARMY GROUP CENTER
Second Panzer Army
TULA
13th Army
BRYANSK FRONT
Bryansk
Starodub
Orel
3rd Army
Tambov
Desna
Elets
Second Army
Chernigov
Kursk
40th Army
Voronezh
21st Army
Romny
Sixth Army
Korotoyak
SOUTHWESTERN FRONT
38th Army
KHARKOV
Poltava
6th Army
57th Army
Kazansk
Balakleya
9th Army
Dnepr
Krasnograd
Izium
Lozovaia
37th Army
Elisavetgrad
Pavlograd
Slaviansk
Donets
Voroshilovgrad
Ekaterinoslav
Seventeenth Army
12th Army
ARMY GROUP SOUTH
Stalino
18th Army
First Panzer Army
56th Army
Dnepr
Don
Nikolayev
ROSTOV
Berdyansk
TRANS-CAUCASIAN FRONT
Perekop
SEA OF AZOV
51st Army
Taman
Simferopol
Kerch
Ekaterinodar
Theodosia
Sevastopol
44th Army
BLACK SEA
0 50 100 150 km
Front line April 1942
Front line Dec 1942
Soviet advance

The Soviets lost many of their armored trains during the summer of 1942. The destruction of a bridge was responsible for the loss of this train. Somehow, the train has managed to stay balanced (for the most part).

fight until the end, defending each block, each house. The arterial routes of the town were cleared fairly quickly, but the Soviets clung to the smaller streets and the large squares, which they transformed into buffer zones. The panzers themselves couldn't risk entering the built-up area for fear of being destroyed. Several buildings had been turned into armed fortresses, including the central post office and the NKVD (Communist secret police) headquarters. Colonel Reinhardt, commander of the 421st Infantry Regiment (Swabian), described the Soviet defense:

> It was the NKVD troops and pioneer troops who barricaded Rostov, and who would defend the city until the last cartridge, which was significant. These protectors of the Bolshevik regime, Stalin's SS, the backbone of both the state and secret police, were some sort of an elite force: excellent soldiers, fanatics, hard and cruel, up to date with all ruses of war and blindly obedient. They were old masters of street combat; their essential purpose, as supporters of the regime, was to repress any possible subversive manifestations.

Rostov-on-Don, "gateway to the Caucasus," was fought over during the Russian Civil War—at that time it was the most industrialized city in southern Russia. During World War II the city would be fought over three times. In 1941 the First Panzer Army took the city, but were driven out by the 37th Soviet Army; in July 1942 the Germans would take it again, and hold it until February 1943 when the Red Army would retake the city. It took a decade to restore the city after the war.

> What these specialists did in Rostov was inconceivable: they tore up the streets and used the cobblestones to make barricades several meters thick. The crossroads were barred by blockhouses. Chevaux de frise and mines made any approach impossible. The doors of the houses were bricked up, the windows had been stacked with sandbags to turn them into arrow slits, and the balconies

# In Profile:
# German Light Panzers and Armored Vehicles

The light Panzer II played an important role in the invasions of Poland and France, and even though it was being superseded by the Panzer III and IV, large numbers of Panzer IIs were still in use at the launch of *Barbarossa.*

A Panzer II C of 11th Panzer Division during the advance on Stalingrad in July 1942. This vehicle was unusual, the type F being the most commonly used within this unit. Moreover, the divisionary tactical symbol on the side has replaced the famous "ghost."

A Russian BA-20 M recovered by a German military police unit. This kind of vehicle, unsuitable for service at the front, helped to protect key routes, as partisan attacks on convoys traveling along the German supply lines were becoming more and more troublesome. The colors and markings on this armored car are a recreation. The 16th Panzer Division also used these vehicles (Lt. Rinschen).

Panzer II F of 2 Company/Staff, 14th Panzer Division. This type of tank, obsolete after 1940, was still used in part by the German panzer divisions during the third year of the war. Its role was to take infantry over long distances and clear small points of enemy resistance.

An SdKfz 7, towing a 150mm gun, pushes through powdery snow. On its mudguard is a complicated tactical insignia, designating this ensemble as forming part of a battery of towed heavy guns. (Bundesarchiv)

> had become machine-gun nests. Well-camouflaged elite snipers had taken up positions on the roofs, while the cellars were stocked with tens of thousands of Molotov cocktails … If a door was left unbricked, it was because a mine had been hidden inside to take out anyone who might try to enter. …
>
> The fighting for the center of Rostov was merciless. The defenders would not surrender; they were going to fight to their last breath; though injured, they kept on firing until they themselves were shot down. We had to put our own injured in armored cars and under guard, so we wouldn't return to find them massacred.[1]

To finish off their determined enemies, the Germans only used a few tanks (unsuited as they were to the style of combat), and instead attacked with grenades and flame-throwers, destroying the balconies and barricades with their 75mm infantry howitzers. This allowed them to take control of Rostov within 50 hours.

## Another Change of Direction

On July 23, Hitler outlined his plans for Operation *Brunswick*, the conquest of the Caucasus, in his Directive no. 45. List's Army Group A received the order to destroy the enemy to the south and south-east of Rostov, then to occupy the entire coast of the Black Sea, and finally to eliminate the Russian fleet. This objective became a priority, with the capture of the oilfields relegated to an annex. Still, List received the order to seize Maykop and Grozny simultaneously, and to prepare to, finally, march on Baku. This change in objective forced List to divide his troops so he could attack from two very different directions: the south, along the Black Sea, and east in the direction of the Caspian Sea. The question arises as to why Hitler suddenly considered the capture of the Russian fleets' ports a pressing necessity. Perhaps he feared a Soviet landing to the rear of Army Group South. Moreover, the political

1 Bergström, Christer. *Operation Barbarossa 1941: Hitler against Stalin*. Philadelphia: Casemate, 2016, pp.466–467.

Despite being beaten very soundly, the Red Army actually lost fewer soldiers to captivity than they had the previous year. (Bundesarchiv)

aspect of the conquest of the Caucasus, especially concerning Turkey, which he hoped would enter the war on his side, cannot be ignored.

The same directive—no. 45—fixed the objectives of Army Group B, led by von Weichs: the capture of Stalingrad, followed by an advance along the Volga as far as Astrakhan.

This poor-quality photograph is valuable as it was taken during combat. An armored group, comprising Panzer IIIs and IVs, motorcycles and at least one eight-wheeled reconnaissance vehicle (an SdKfz 232 or 263), is attacking a Soviet strongpoint, established inside a village. (Bundesarchiv)

A Sturmgechütz II or 40 crosses a river at a ford, in front of a retrenchment made from sacks of earth. (Bundesarchiv)

## The Two Adversaries Prepare for Battle

To carry out his offensive, List separated Army Group A into two tactical groups: Group Ruoff, with the Seventeenth Army (five German infantry divisions) and the 3rd Romanian Army (one infantry and three cavalry divisions); and First Panzer Army, with three panzer divisions, two motorized divisions, four infantry divisions, and the Slovak Fast Division.

At first look, it appears that von Kleist's First Panzer Army was the more powerful of the two, but in reality the three panzer divisions had no more than 400 functioning tanks between them, and Group Ruoff would later be reinforced by XXXXII Army Corps on their return from the Crimea. This army corps was essentially composed of Romanian troops.

List had planned to use the railroad from Rostov to Baku to supply the advancing troops. However delays were caused by the bottleneck at the Rostov junction, and the different Russian rail gauges. The delays meant that the German forces were constantly short of fuel, which strangled the operations' chances of success.

Group Ruoff was tasked with capturing the entire coast of the Black Sea, while the First Panzer Army had to take Voroshilovsk, Grozny, and Baku. Even before the offensive began, List was worried about the terrain his troops would have to cross. It was over 1,200 km from Rostov to Baku, which would create an extremely long front to be protected towards the south. The Caucasian mountains, whose summits peaked at 4,500 m, would be very difficult to negotiate. And before they reached the mountains, List's men would have to cross the Don and the swamps south of Rostov, before entering a rich region, which in turn gave way to an arid steppe. Their progress would be made even more difficult by their lack of

Malinovsky's Southern Front had numerous tanks of British and American origin, which came through Iran. These mostly comprised American tanks such as this Stuart, a standard M3 with a riveted hull. The anti-aircraft machine gun has been removed. (Bundesarchiv)

fuel and vehicles. As far as the Red Army was concerned, the first line was held by Rodion Malinovky's Southern Front, which had suffered greatly, though had maintained its cohesion. Several divisions were reduced to a few hundred men and, worse, the lines of communication, trains, and services had been totally shaken up and were impossible to repair, especially as the civilian population had fled to the south and east, taking their carts, livestock, and farm machinery with them. Three armies had been withdrawn from the front line and were being re-formed in the interior of the country, which left the 18th and 37th Armies opposite the Don. To their right were the 12th and 51st Armies of Budyonny's North Caucasian Front, whose reserve amounted to just the 47th Army, the 17th Cossack Cavalry Corps and a few infantry corps. The Trans-Caucasian Front, guarding the Turkish and Iranian borders against the Germans, protected Grozny and Baku, and therefore the Caucasian mountains.

For the first time since the war in the east had begun, the balance of aerial forces went in the Russians' favor; the Germans had only IV Air Corps, two Ju 87 Stuka squadrons, and three fighter squadrons in place. The Russians had superior numbers, if we are to believe

A Valentine pierced by 88mm shells, mirroring the fate of its British counterparts destroyed during the battle of Ruweisat at the exact same time on July 23, 1942. (Bundesarchiv)

# In Profile:
# German and Romanian Messerschmitt 109s

A Bf 109 F4 belonging to the commander of the Blue Squadron, composed of Spanish volunteers, mostly veterans of the Spanish Civil War. Captain Noriega, whose aircraft is shown here, was shot down after his eighth sortie on July 1, 1942. The Spanish were credited with one victory—an LaGG 3.

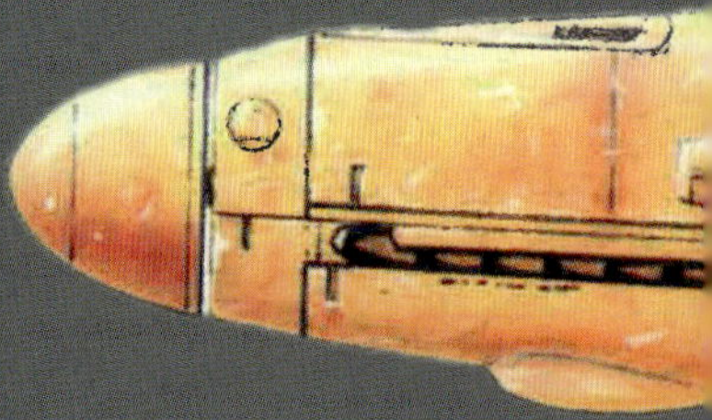

Insignia of the III/JG 52

A Bf 109 F4 from the 9/JG 52. This aircraft belonged to Hermann Graf, the first pilot to exceed 200 aerial victories, which he achieved in 13 months on the Eastern Front. Graf's specialty was "jumping hurdles," a technique by which he got rid of most of his adversaries, usually pilots of Lavochkin 5 or 7. Graf, by the end of the conflict, had shot down several B-17s from the 8th Army Air Force, while fighting above the Reich. His aircraft is shown here as it appeared during his 108th victory, in May 1942, in the skies over the Crimea.

A Bf 109 E from the Romanian air army. The pilots allied to the Germans—Hungarians, Romanians, Italians, and Finns—accounted for no fewer than 16,000 aerial victories on all fronts. Their role, too often forgotten by most historians, remained important during this conflict, even taking into account their often outdated equipment and small number of pilots engaged.

*Above:* An insignia seen on a Romanian Me 109 E, meaning unknown.

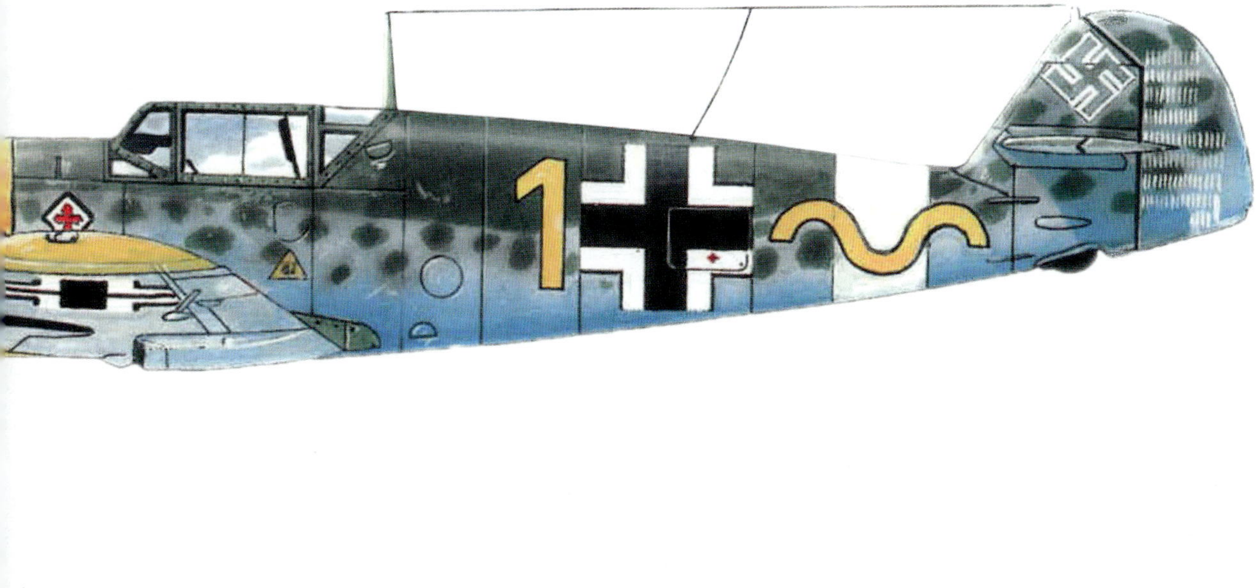

Despite the high temperature, the rivers had not dried up and engineers were often forced to intervene. These two SdKfz 251s have been painted a light color to make them less visible—1942 marked the end of the panzer-gray camouflage widely used during the first years of the war. (Bundesarchiv)

the majority of authors on the subject, who unfortunately do not give specific numbers. A sergeant of 14th Panzer Division described his arrival at the Don, around July 23:

> We got to the Don only to find most of the bridges down, but very little sign of the enemy. The heat was stifling ... the whole length of the right bank was smothered in dust clouds as more and more vehicles began to pile up there. Russian resistance was so slight that many of the soldiers were able to take off their clothes and bathe—as we had in the Dnieper exactly a year ago. Let us hope that history does not repeat itself!
>
> We were there for two days while the engineers were working. We suffered a good deal of attention from Russian aircraft; they would come over singly and in pairs at dusk, and at first light when the Luftwaffe was absent. In places Russian artillery was quite strong ... they could be heard at night moving the guns into position, and would bombard us when the sun rose ... its flat rays from the east showed our positions in detail, but made it difficult to spot their muzzle flashes.[2]

## Malinovsky Cannot Resist

On July 25, 1942, List attacked from three bridgeheads on the Don. The Southern Front was obliterated, incapable of resisting the German pressure. Contrary to a well-established legend, even among historians such as Paul Carell, there was never an order from the Stavka authorizing Russian troops to retreat inside the country to better destroy the adversary there. On the contrary, the only defensive policy adopted was that of resistance, without thought of retreat. In his order no. 227, dated July 28, 1942, Stalin indicated that no more than one "step back" would be tolerated, so it was very unlikely that they were implementing a new tactic. If the Soviets did retreat here, it was only because they were incapable of standing their ground, unlike the previous year when the troops had been fresh and well-equipped.

2 Clark, Alan. *Barbarossa: The Russian German Conflict 1941–1945*. London: Weidenfeld & Nicolson, 1995.

Opposite the First Panzer Army, the 12th and 37th Armies were forced to retreat quickly. The 51st Army, witnessing the approach of Hoth's Fourth Panzer Army, which held the south wing of the Army Group B, and First Panzer Army, which formed the north wing of Army Group A, was in a difficult situation, faced with being encircled and destroyed. It retreated to the northeast to rejoin the Stalingrad Front, losing contact with its original front, that of General Malinovsky.

On July 28, the Southern Front was in such a state that it had to be absorbed into the North Caucasian Front. The latter, still under the command of Budyonny, was divided into two tactical groups: the Don group (Malinovsky), whose 37th and 12th Armies, exhausted, had to attempt to contain von Kleist's advance towards Grozny, and the coastal group, with the 18th, 47th, and 56th Armies, the Cossack Cavalry Corps and an infantry corps. Each group was supported by an aerial army.

The Russian aerial superiority was not enough to slow down the German advance, whose rapidity was surprising particularly given the unfavorable geographical and climatic conditions. The men and the horses, despite suffering from the overwhelming heat and terrible thirst, advanced 50 kilometers per day, day after day, without rest. The panzers and the trucks were continually brought to a standstill due to lack of fuel, which was delivered to the front line by various means, including by camel.

At the beginning of August, Maykop was under direct threat and the crews began to dismantle their oil installations. But the German advance was too fast, and the Russians were forced to destroy them instead of evacuating them. On August 5, Voroshilovsk (now Stavropol) was taken and the next day, the 1st Independent Infantry Corps was crushed. The 12th and 18th Armies could not then contain the First Panzer Army and retreated towards the Caucasian mountains, opening the road to Maykop, which was captured almost immediately. Most of the oil silos were, by that point, on fire, but the pits themselves had been spared. Similarly, the rail node had been taken but the rolling stock had been moved just

This Panzer II is preparing to cross a bridge built by German pathfinders. (Bundesarchiv)

A Junkers Ju 52 in the Caucasus. This type of transportation aircraft was very frequently used during the campaign of summer 1942, as resupply missions could not keep up with demand, and aerial intervention was often essential. This Ju 52/53 m is particularly streamlined, with its nose cap (rare at the time) and wheel fairings. This aircraft may have belonged to an important individual—note the pennant beside the windscreen. It also has an insignia with a crown surmounting a shield, partly hidden here by the propeller. (Bundesarchiv)

a few wrecks remained. The Russians made considerable efforts to reinforce the Caucasian Front. First, they raised new units in Georgia, Azerbaijan, and Armenia. Second, they sent large numbers of reinforcements and heavy armaments by rail to Astrakhan, then by sea to Baku. This town, like Grozny, was surrounded by several successive lines of defense, including a moat that had been created by diverting mountain torrents through the efforts of the Red Army's engineers and conscripted civilians.

## The Summit of Mount Elbrus

Meanwhile the Seventeenth Army progressed southwards, seizing Krasnodar. The battle on the Taman Peninsula, however, was brutal. The Soviets did not want to lose Novorossiysk—their last large naval base on the Black Sea—without good reason.

The journey along the coastline was problematic due to the sheer fury of the 47th Army and the naval infantry brigades, so the Germans tried to approach the large port by crossing the Caucasian mountains, which the Russian commander considered impenetrable. On August 18, XXXXVIV Mountain Corps managed to clear a passage through the mountains and two divisions from Group Ruoff, the 73rd and the 125th Infantry Divisions, reached the sea exactly as Xenophon said the Greeks had 2,400 years earlier—shouting *'Thalassa! Thalassa!'* But on August 28, 1942, the situation was much changed: it hadn't been a sign of deliverance for the Germans following a tortuous journey through the mountains, but the premises of a violent battle. Novorossiysk was surrounded the following week, and reduced by the 73rd Infantry Division between September 6 and 10.

With Novorossiysk conquered, the next objectives were Tuapse, Sokhom, and Batumi, on the Turkish border. Progress through the coastal zone still being difficult, the German mountain corps returned to the mountains. This time, the peaks were very high, situated between 2,000 and 3,000 meters above sea level. The 1st and 4th Mountain Divisions were engaged in battle to try and conquer them, so they could appear behind the Russians at Sokhom, just 160 km from Batumi and the Turkish border. To protect the flanks of these two divisions, a company of guides and mountain troops were sent to Mount Elbrus. They could not stop themselves from asking their general for authorization to scale the 5,633-meter mountain. They accomplished the climb on August 21, 1942, and around 29 men of the 1st and 4th Mountain Divisions planted a swastika flag on the mountain's summit, beside the standards of both divisions. This was a great physical accomplishment that the German propaganda machine jumped on enthusiastically, but it was not followed by military success on the ground, as the Kampfgruppe Stettner, comprising two battalions of 91st Jäger Regiment, only got within 20 km of Sokhom: the troops were exhausted, too few in number, and deprived of any support; they had only two mountain guns with 25 shells per piece.

The city of Novorossiysk is the main Russian port on the Black Sea, and is one of the 12 cities of the Soviet Union that was awarded with the honorary title of Hero City due to outstanding heroism during World War II. The battle to take the port was tough and lasted nearly three weeks. Eventually the center of the town was captured on September 8, and Ruoff ordered V Army Corps to continue along the coast road. The road was held by three battalions of Soviet naval infantrymen and some surviving soldiers, who had established positions in factories. Despite repeated attacks, the larger German forces could not dislodge the Soviets.

A group of Soviet sailors held part of the town from February 1943 until the town was liberated. Their defense of the port meant that the Germans couldn't use the port to ship supplies.

Reinforcements would allow them to complete their objective, and they waited for several days for the Italian *Alpini*. But they never arrived: they had been diverted to Stalingrad. Sokhom was never captured, nor was Tuapse, 50 kilometers ahead of the 97th Jäger Division's vanguard.

# Towards the Caspian Sea

At the beginning of September, von Kleist's First Panzer Army found itself 100 km from Grozny and 500 km from Baku. The Caspian Sea itself was close and 16th Motorized Infantry Division was sent in the direction of Astrakhan. The division hurried over the Kalmuck steppe as far as Elista. In mid-September, four patrols were sent on a long-range recon mission, as aviation reconnaissance wasn't possible. Their mission was two-fold: to

1. discover if the enemy had concentrated its forces at the breach between the Tcherek and the Volga, if he had undertaken to cross the latter river and in this case where his points of reference were, and if troop movements were taking place on the Stalingrad–Astrakhan road
2. reconnoiter the maritime traffic conditions, the Caspian Sea coast, the west bank of the Volga, and also the new railroad line between Kizlyar and Astrakhan, whose route was yet unknown.

The reconnaissance groups comprised two eight-wheeler SdKfz 232 armored cars; a 24-man section of motorcyclists; two 50 mm Pak guns mounted on an armored chassis; a group of engineers with their equipment, in two trucks; two trucks loaded with fuel and water; a truck for the commissariat; a repair truck; and a medical car.

These patrols advanced towards the east. Lieutenant Euler's patrol came within 7 km of the Volga delta, 35 km from Astrakhan, while that of Lieutenant Schliep discovered the Kizlyar–Astrakhan railroad at the Senseli station. This railroad, used by large cargo trains carrying oil and fuel from Baku and Grozny, was not on German maps, as it had only been built very recently. Schliep surprised a convoy and set fire to it in its entirety with his two SdKfz 232s, before the engineering team blew up the tracks and the group retreated.

These four patrols all reported the same information: there were very few Soviet troops on the Kalmuck steppe and no counteroffensive was to be feared for the moment from Astrakhan, where the Russian positions were purely defensive. The town was defended by a newly created army, the 28th.

Due to a lack of paint, the crew of this SdKfz 250 are camouflaging their vehicle with mud. (Bundesarchiv)

# The Final Effort towards Baku and Grozny

On August 25, the Germans decided to cross the Tcherek River in order to seize the oil fields at Malgobek and Ordzhonikidze. They had to act quickly—the German units had been replenished, but Soviet reinforcements were also now arriving in the sector—not only men who had come from central Russia or the Caucasian regions, but also brand-new materiel, brought from America via Iran. The situation was already worrying, as the Germans only had eight divisions available for their new attack, compared to the Soviets' 40: XXXX Panzer Corps, with three armored divisions, against Grozny, towards the east; LII Army Corps, with four infantry divisions, against Malgobek and Ordzhonikidzy, towards the south; and III Panzer Corps, with one Romanian mountain division and a German *kampfgruppe*, towards the south, to cut the military routes to Batumi and Tiflis.

On August 30, First Panzer Army crossed the Tcherek, but they encountered determined resistance. The Russian counterattacks, violent and repeated, prevented any advance towards Grozny and the bulk of the German effort was therefore directed south. Yet the 9th and 37th Armies refused to surrender, and after two days of heavy losses on both sides, von Kleist was forced onto the defensive. The capital of Chechnya was therefore never captured by the Germans, nor was Baku, the center of the Soviet oil industry. The consequences for the two generals that Hitler viewed as responsible for the failure—List and Halder, OKH chief of staff—were unpleasant. On September 7, the Führer sent Chief of Operations of the OKW, Alfred Jodl, to List's command post, to investigate why the offensive had been halted. On

This SdKfz 251 on the Kalmuck steppe has been camouflaged with light-colored paint. (Bundesarchiv)

# In Profile:
# Panzer III H, J, and SdKfz 263

A Panzer III H from the 16th Panzer Division, which took part in the advance on Stalingrad. Like a good number of other armored vehicles of this type used by the 24th Panzer Division, it has a catchall box at the rear.

The rear box and "Rommel Kiste" of another Panzer III of the 24th Panzer Division.

An SdKfz 263 from the 13th Panzer Division, part of a reconnaissance group. The 13th Panzer Division was one of the few German divisions to use the same tactical symbols throughout the war.

A Panzer III J of the 24th Panzer Division with a 50mm short gun. The armor plate appears to have been added later, the unit hardly having been provided with it. The division's traditional insignia, a knight, honors its previous form as a cavalry division.

The German army's advance continued, but the lines of communication were incredibly stretched and the fighters on the front line were no longer numerous enough—nor did they have enough equipment and munitions—to win the day, even though Grozny and Baku were close by. This SdKfz 222 is armed with a 2.8cm PzB anti-tank gun, easily recognizable even though hidden by a tarp. (Bundesarchiv)

A team of German machine gunners shelter behind an SdKfz 250 and a light T-70 or T-70A Russian tank. The latter is armed with a 45mm gun, which gave it a greater firepower than the T-60. In addition, the frontal armor of the T-70 was around 45mm thick. (Bundesarchiv)

Autumn and winter arrived quickly in the Caucasus. In this photograph, mud is clearly visible on the tracks. The only tank retaining its panzer-gray paint is 923, a Panzer III Ausf. J. Its unit is unknown, but on its gun a small tactical insignia can be made out, which suggests it belonged to the general staff of a panzer regiment or 2nd Panzer Battalion. (Bundesarchiv)

his return, Jodl sided with List, saying that he had only been obeying the orders that Hitler himself had given. He then cited the orders in question. This was too much for Hitler, who lost his temper, swearing that he had never given those orders before storming out of the conference room.

After this outburst, the Führer made several decisions. No longer having confidence in any of his generals (Jodl was one of the most submissive, incidentally), he refused to share even one more meal with them, until the end of the war, preferring to lock himself in alone. This could be seen as anecdotal, but his other measures were considerably less so: ordering the immediate return of List and Halder. Coming as it did after the dismissal of Walther von Brauchitsch, the commander-in-chief of the army in late 1941, Halder's departure tightened Hitler's grip on the Heer. He also decided to separate himself from his two most loyal servants in the OKW—Generals Keitel and Jodl—and to replace them with Kesselring and Paulus, but gave up on this. The two men stayed in their positions, but from now on, all meetings had to be recorded in shorthand, so there would be tangible proof of everything that was decided. This was, incidentally, excellent news for historians.

# A Final Success

From the middle of September, the weather became considerably colder in the Caucasus and it soon became evident that the German objectives would not be accomplished in 1942. However, on October 25, two panzer divisions (13th and 23rd Panzer Divisions) of III Panzer Corps launched a surprise attack in the direction of Ordzhonikidze, with the support of IV Air Corps. Seven divisions of the 37th Soviet Army were crushed and routed, losing 16,000 prisoners, 249 guns, and 188 tanks. On November 2, von Kleist's tanks were 5 kilometers from the oil city, but the snow began to fall, and a Soviet counterattack cut the 13th Panzer Division off from the German lines. Only a joint attack by the 13th Panzer Division on one side, and the SS-Wiking Division from outside the pocket, saved the armored unit.

On the First Panzer Army's front, the operations had concluded. The objectives assigned had not been achieved, except for Maykop, which was only of lesser importance. Von Kleist would justify this after the war by stressing the complete lack through the campaign of two essential elements of modern warfare: fuel and aerial support:

> The primary cause of our failure was shortage of petrol. The bulk of our supplies had to come by rail from the Rostov bottleneck, as the Black Sea route was considered unsafe. A certain amount of oil was delivered by air, but the total which came through was insufficient to maintain the momentum of the advance, which came to a halt just when our chances looked best.
>
> But that was not the ultimate cause of the failure. We could still have reached our goal if my forces had not been drawn away bit by bit to help the attack at Stalingrad. Besides part of my motorized troops, I had to give up the whole of my flak corps and all my air force except the reconnaissance squadrons.

The remains of a T-60 hit by a huge shell—probably 88mm. (Bundesarchiv)

German infantry attacks a farm, where Russian defenders have probably entrenched themselves. Despite success in October 1942, the Germans couldn't progress any further through the Caucasus with winter looming. (Bundesarchiv)

With the autumn came the cold—these men and their officer have just finished setting up an MG 34 machine gun wearing thick woolen gloves. (Bundesarchiv)

Behind the shelter of an SdKfz 250, these men from a reconnaissance unit rest during the advance on Stalingrad. Despite their tiredness, they seem in good spirits. (Bundesarchiv)

It should be noted at this point that the so-called oil brigades sent by the Germans—10,000 men in all—were not able to exploit the oil wells conquered in the Caucasus, because of Soviet sabotage.

While the advance in the Caucasus remained a great feat for the German army, none of the final objectives had been achieved: they had taken control neither of the Caspian Sea nor the Baku oil, which continued to be sent to the rest of the USSR. Nor had they conquered the Black Sea coast, from where the Russian navy controlled the seas, while Axis forces had only six small U-boats, and the Turks retained control over shipping through the Dardanelles Straits.

# The Advance on Stalingrad

In the plans for Case *Blau*, Stalingrad was a sidenote to the principal operations. But little by little, both the Germans and Russians became obsessed with the city and decided to go all-out in their efforts to control it.

At the beginning of July, during the initial phase of the German offensive, Sixth Army was the largest element of Army Group South, with five corps, totaling 18 divisions, including two armored and one motorized (which formed XXXX Panzer Corps). Though Sixth Army was arguably the most powerful, its main weakness was its limited mobility.

After the capture of Voronezh, Paulus's army advanced along the Don quite slowly due to its lack of support. Next, Hoth's Fourth Panzer Army met up with Sixth Army at the end of July, but its forces were not very impressive: one sole panzer division, a motorized division, and two infantry divisions. Following at the rear were six Romanian infantry divisions. The group was supported by VIII Air Corps, which consisted of three *Stukageschwader*, nine *Jagdsgeschwader*, and nine *Kampfgeschwader*.

## The Red Army in Crisis

The division of the old Army Group South into Army Group A and Army Group B did not improve the coordination of the German troops or the supply and transport situation. These were decided at the OKH itself, by the quartermaster general, General Eduard Wagner, who robbed Peter to pay Paul according to Hitler's changes in priorities. So, the bulk of the supplies were transferred to Army Group A, in the south, to meet Hitler's demands. This had the consequence of stopping Paulus for at least 10 days (18 according to Paul Carell).

This delay proved a boon for the Soviets, who were allowed some breathing space and time to organize the defense of the Don loop to the west. Many reinforcements were sent to this area to strengthen what remained of Timoshenko's front. The new arrivals were stunned—shocked, even—by the state of the divisions and general staff of the vanquished army. General Vasily Chuikov, commander of the reserve army, gives us several examples in his memoirs, notably when his first elements arrived on the Stalingrad Front, created on July 12, and the chief of staff on the front in question ordered his men to take a position by carrying out a forced 200-kilometer march:

> It was impossible to execute such orders in the prescribed time conditions; especially since part of the army elements that had to execute them had not yet arrived. The Chief of Staff told me that the orders had to be obeyed, but that he would think about it; and in the end, he told me to come back and see him the next day.

Paulus's Sixth Army didn't count on having a lot of armored divisions, but the units of Sturmgeschütz III and 40 had a good number of tanks. In this photo, StuG IIIs charge across the countryside in a cloud of dust. (Bundesarchiv)

> The following morning, however, he wasn't at the command post, and no-one could tell me where he could be. What to do? I went to see the chief of the operations section, Colonel Ruckle. I showed him that the mission I had been given was impossible to execute within the time limits and asked him to report to the Front's military council that the 64th Army could only occupy the positions assigned to us by July 23rd at the earliest.
>
> Ruckle reacted quickly: without referring to anyone, changed the date listed for the occupation of the defensive line by hand from July 21st to July 23rd. How could the head of an operations section, without even speaking to his general, change a date relating to operations? Who was commanding the front?[1]
>
> During a personal reconnaissance, I fell on two divisions' general staffs … if one could call so-called groups of officers moving in four or five trucks' overload of barrels and cans of gasoline "divisions." I asked them where the Germans were and what we knew of their movements, without being able to get a valid answer … It was clear that restoring in these men the faith that they had lost in their own strength, and improving the militant virtues of units exhausted by retirement, would not be an easy task.

The 21st Army's command post was not to Chuikov's taste:

> The entire general staff was on wheels; transmissions, supplies, all were on or in trucks; I appreciated this luxury of mobility little. In all things there appeared a lack of firmness in resistance and little ardor in combat. It was felt that everyone inside this office, from the general commanding the army to the commanders, stood constantly at-the-ready to escape the pursuit.

1 General Chuikov, *The Beginning of the Road.* Moscow: Progress Publishers, various editions. Each front was in principle commanded by a military council, which was composed of the general, his chief of staff and a political commissar. At the Stalingrad Front, therefore, the general was Gordov, successor to Timoshenko, the chief of staff, Nikitchev, from July 24, and the political commissar, Nikita Khrushchev.

The commander of the Stalingrad Front, General Vasily Gordov, was himself in an uncertain position, as his unit was soon divided in two—a new Stalingrad Front, of which he retained command, and a Southeastern Front, which was placed under the command of General Andrey Yeremenko.

Yeremenko got along badly with Gordov from the start, and used his intimacy with Khrushchev to plot against him, eventually managing to get him sacked. Gordov's main fault was that he did not listen to either the political commissars or the military councils. He wanted to make decisions alone, and wrote to Stalin the next year, when he was commanding the 33rd Army, asking for the abolition of the military councils, which he saw as "useless and a waste of time." Stalin, unlike Hitler, valued the experience of his generals; he left Gordov in office, and the general later played a key role in the capture of Berlin under the command of Koniev. But in 1946, while he was head of the Volga military district, the communist dictator had him removed.

In July 1942, Chuikov described Gordov thus:

> His hair had turned gray; his tired eyes gave the impression that they saw nothing, and their cold regard seemed to say: "No need to tell me about the situation, I know it already; but given the events, I feel I cannot do a thing."

A "militarized" agricultural tractor that seems to have returned to its original purpose in a peaceful Russian village. (Bundesarchiv)

Two views of a Lee tank still bearing its American registration number (USA W 304850), with a turret number added by the Russians (147) and carrying German national symbols. According to the hand-written inscription on the glacis plate, it is about to be sent to Germany to be studied by specialists in the OKW. (Bundesarchiv)

Tank combat became more frequent and more dogged as Sixth Army approached Stalingrad. The Soviets launched into battle with the very last T-34 model, the T-34/76D, recognizable from its larger and less contoured turret.

# The Battle of Kalach

On July 20, 1942, Paulus resumed his advance, launching a battle of encirclement with the aim of destroying six Soviet infantry divisions and several tank units—the 62nd and 64th Armies—and the new 1st and 4th Tank Armies, which were far from at their full force—just 240 tanks according to Soviet General Rokossovsky—and poorly trained. This figure of 240 tanks appears to be an underestimation; the Germans counted more than this on the field after the battle.

The Germans attacked in a pincer movement, with XIV Panzer Corps to the left and XXIV Panzer Corps to the right. The lead unit of the XIV Panzer Corps was the 24th Panzer Division. It took three days of tough fighting to push the front of the 64th Army back south of the sector, cross the Chir (on the evening of July 26), and drive towards the Don, which they reached at daybreak on July 27. This night advance surprised the Russians, who nonetheless managed to completely destroy their bridge over the river. The Germans repaired it quickly and moved elements over to the east of the Don, just 70 kilometers from Stalingrad. But it would have been madness to continue in this direction without reducing the Kalach pocket. For the first time since the beginning of the campaign, the Soviets stopped running and seemed determined to fight.

To the north of the attack front, the 16th Panzer Division succeeded in breaking through and found themselves just 10 kilometers from Kalach when the 1st Tank Army counterattacked.

Two formidable adversaries of Russian tanks advance towards Stalingrad: a Panzer IV Ausf. F2 in the foreground and a Sturmgeschütz 40 in the background. This kind of terrain was perfectly suited to large armored maneuvers. (Bundesarchiv)

The battle that followed was fierce and indecisive. For several days, the tanks tried to break out and encircle each other, seeking rare dominant positions in the steppe, engaged in a merciless fight while under constant fire from both German and Russian aircraft. Kampfgruppe Krumpen was surrounded and the delivery of supplies was terribly difficult because, once again, the 16th Panzer Division did not have sufficient supplies of fuel. It required the intervention of Junkers Ju 52s, who dropped fuel supplies, to get them moving again and relieve the *kampfgruppe*. Elsewhere, the Soviets did not see the same success: Kampfgruppe Reinisch destroyed 67 of 200 tanks that attacked them.

The problem of supplies was acute, as seen from the war diary of Air Fleet 4:

> **August 2, 1942: Sixth Army are no longer advancing towards Stalingrad because of the increased resistance of the enemy, but moreover because of the lack of supplies. Russia still attacked in places ... The Russians are throwing everything they can scrape up into Stalingrad. The VIII Air Corps will support Sixth Army in front of Stalingrad. It will attack traffic on the railroads and rivers and make supply flights for this army.**
>
> **August 7, 1942: The Führer ordered us to charge the bridgehead at Kalach. The reinforced VIII Air Corps and Sixth Army were there. Paulus full of confidence ...**
>
> **August 10, 1942: with the aim of taking control of the situation, von R[ichthofen] has made the following decisions: Air CG: Stalingrad. The exploration squadrons will immediately deliver 3,000 tonnes of supplies. A Flak division will be sent immediately to Stalingrad, as will all columns available to the Air Fleet 4.**[2]

Von Richthofen was perhaps somewhat optimistic when he spoke of Stalingrad as if Paulus was there already. This was still not the case by August 10. Days before, the situation had improved, when 16th and 24th Panzer Divisions met at Kalach, closing the crucible lid on the entire 62nd Army, eight infantry divisions, and the equivalent of 10 tank brigades, according to the war diary of Halder himself.

2 Cited by Walter Gorlitz in Beevor, Anthony. *Stalingrad*. New York: Viking, 1998, p. 186.

This T-34/76D was destroyed or abandoned just in front of an embankment used by German troops. A mortar tube lies on the ground. This photo allows us to see the various differences between the turret of the 76D and its predecessors, the 76B and C: apart from the characteristic more angular shape, the biggest change is the replacement of the single turret roof hatch with two smaller, circular ones. This type of tank is sometimes called model 1943, but its official Soviet designation is T-34 06 42/43. (Bundesarchiv)

The Russians refused to surrender, conforming to Stalin's directive of neither retreating nor relenting. The battle was therefore far from over, and it took 15 days to clear the Kalach pocket. The Red Army lost 35,000 men, killed or taken prisoner, as well as 270 tanks and 600 guns. It was one of the few encirclement battles that the Germans had succeeded in implementing since the beginning of the summer offensive. It was completed with heavy losses inflicted on both tank armies. More than 13,000 Russian soldiers were captured, but with an energy born of desperation, the Soviets stood their ground in a bridgehead west of the Don, south of Kremensk. The Germans took little notice; they had already wasted enough time around Kalach and wanted to capitalize on their victory by moving quickly against Stalingrad—an altogether bigger fish than this little bridgehead. But it was from this bridgehead that one of the pincers of Russia's victorious winter counteroffensive would launch.

At the time, the preservation of this small pocket to the west of the Don was little consolation for the Red Army. The Stalingrad Front was now in a worrying condition, reduced to 38 divisions; half of these counted around 6,000–8,000 men per division, while the other half had barely 1,000 men each. Just 360 tanks and 330 planes were in fighting form. However, aside from one small German bridgehead, the Soviets still held the entire east bank of the Don. Sixth Army, therefore, would have to force their way across the river.

The Germans claimed that they destroyed one thousand Soviet tanks and 750 guns in the Kalach pocket, though this is probably an exaggeration. Of course the battle also caused German losses. The success at Kalach raised German hopes for the swift capture of Stalingrad. However by mid-August, Paulus's armored forces had already lost half their strength, and there were still pockets of Soviet resistance remaining.

This T-34/76B was destroyed in the vicinity of Stalingrad, in a neighborhood that experienced fierce fighting. The wreck seems to have served as a form of protection for a shelter directly beneath it. (Bundesarchiv)

## Halder Approaches Stalingrad

South of the Don, Hoth's Fourth Panzer Army repelled the 51st Soviet Army on the Kalmuck steppe, which allowed them to strike at the 64th Army from the south. Chuikov's forces reacted violently: these were fresh units who were itching to let rip. Three infantry divisions soon counterattacked, with little effect on the Germans but making a huge impact on the 6th Romanian Corps, which was on the verge of collapse until a group of Heer liaison officers reinforced the Romanian staff's resolve. This did not bode well for the future. Nevertheless, the German position was reestablished and Hoth was able to strike out towards Stalingrad, instigating a brutal battle at Tinguta (around 75 kilometers from Stalingrad).

On August 5, the outer defensive line was broken by the panzers, but the ferocious fighting that developed around Tinguta's rail station prevented Hoth from getting any closer to the Volga. It was clear that Hoth was not going to be able to force the Russian defenses until Paulus started to move again.

The fighting that took place in August 1942 is very interesting, retrospectively, as a number of separate German accounts—from the troops as well as the general staff—indicate a certain loss of impetus. Take, for example, this extract from Air Fleet 4's war diary:

> **August 20, 1942: von Richthofen had another discussion with Paulus about the situation and his intentions. No new attack before the 23rd. Our main job is to fire on the armored vehicles! Paulus is worried about his left flank.**
>
> **August 21, 1942: von Richthofen went to the LI Army Corps with General von Seydliz, who is trying, on the right wing, to form a bridgehead and unblock the tanks.**

A nice shot of a Luftwaffe Kübelwagen alongside a Russian river, more likely the Don than the Volga. This vehicle came from von Richthofen's Air Fleet 4, and it has on its right mudguard a lovely cockerel insignia. (Bundesarchiv)

A Sturmgeschütz 40 and a Panzer III Ausf. J or L advance together towards the top of a hill. The StuG commander seems to be indicating to the vehicles behind him that the path is clear. (Bundesarchiv)

The short 75mm barrel of this SdKfz 251/9 is being energetically cleaned by a member of its crew. Again, the panzer-gray paint job has been updated with daubs of lighter paint. (Bundesarchiv)

The crew of this Panzer III Ausf. J are confident in their victory. An amusing detail: the Rommel kiste cover behind the turret has been padlocked shut. Were there thieves in the Heer? (Bundesarchiv)

Panzers crossing waterways set into desperately flat land. (Bundesarchiv)

"I accompanied a group of scouts …" wrote von Richthofen. "Everything went according to plan. The enemy was much weaker than I expected. The army constantly overestimate their adversary, in reality because the troops are exhausted and don't want to fight any more."

Alan Clark cites a Soviet account, which corroborates that of von Richthofen:

> **The German tanks did not go into action without infantry and air support. On the battlefield there was no evidence of the "prowess" of German tank crews … they operated sluggishly, extremely cautiously and indecisively.**
>
> **The German infantry was strong in automatic fire, but … no rapid movement or resolute attack on the battlefield.**
>
> **When advancing they did not spare their bullets but frequently fired into thin air. Their forward positions, particularly at night, were beautifully visible, being marked by machine-gun fire, tracer bullets, often fired into empty space, and different-colored rockets.[3]**

A Panzer IV Ausf. F2 advances towards Stalingrad. (Bundesarchiv)

3 Alan Clark, *Barbarossa, The Russian German Conflict.*

Sixth Army was essentially non-motorized, and the artillery was therefore horse-drawn, as seen in this photograph. (Bundesarchiv)

## The Assault on the Don

After the terrible defeat suffered on the loop of the Don, General Vasilevsky of the Stavka went to Stalingrad to reorganize the defense. He reconstructed the Stalingrad Front, which grouped together the old front with the same name, with the Southeastern Front. The result, placed under the command of General Yeremenko, consisted of six armies: the 21st, 24th, 63rd, 66th Armies, the 1st and 4th Tank Armies. The 62nd Army was restructured, the others, seriously reorganized and reinforced. Finally, the 51st, 57th, and 64th Armies, though badly battered by the fighting on the Kalmuck steppe and in the loop of the Don, were also refurbished.

The Soviet units did not wait passively; before the German attack against Stalingrad began, on August 23, the Russians attacked their bridgehead to the west of the Don. Their advance was very limited, but they blocked off three infantry divisions and one panzer division. These units, which Paulus deemed absolutely necessary for his advance,

This broken-down Luftwaffe motorcycle and side-car seems to be giving the men trying to repair it a lot of trouble. The insignia on the motorcycle has been seen already, on the Bücker Bestmann in the previous chapter. The bike itself is a DKW NZ 350. (Bundesarchiv)

This SS unit has just installed a mortar in a hastily dug hole. (Bundesarchiv)

were freed thanks to the arrival of General Garibaldi's 8th Italian Army. Mussolini's soldiers found the sector to be anything but a sinecure, as the Russians had multiplied their assaults on the front with their 21st and 63rd Armies, creating a new bridgehead south of the Don.

This Soviet pressure, though it had been contained, worried Paulus before his offensive had even begun. But on August 23, his fears were allayed. The tanks made use of the infantry bridgeheads to charge ahead. Von Wietersheim's XIV Panzer Corps cleared the way for the

A BMW 750 cc R 75 side-car of 24th Panzer Division rolls towards Stalingrad. The white rectangle with a cross, visible on the side, shows that it comes from one of the division's service units. (Bundesarchiv)

A column of Panzer IIIs advance towards the east over completely flat terrain. Note the funnel on the back of the rearmost tank. (Bundesarchiv)

16th Panzer Division, which had come from Westphalia. After having pushing past the precarious defenses of the 62nd Army (mostly thanks to their aerial support), the panzers crossed the anti-tank ditch, the "Tartar trench," and, traversing 60 kilometers in a single day, reached the steep edges of the Volga, north of Stalingrad, where the cliffs overhang the river by about 100 meters. Von Richthofen was triumphant:

These tired men take a moment to rest in the shelter of a small mound covered with wildflowers. German soldiers and Russian prisoners rest side by side, without much visible tension. For the Soviet prisoners, the tragedy would really only commence when they were in the German rear, on the roads to the POW camps and in the camps themselves, where they were treated in a despicable way. (Bundesarchiv)

An SdKfz 7 and its 88mm gun, from the Heer rather than the Luftwaffe, follows a key route near the loop of the Don. (Bundesarchiv)

> **August 23rd, 1942: The VIII Air Corps mobilized the forces of Air Fleet 4 with a stunning rapidity. They literally paralyzed the Russians, and von Wietersheim's tanks jumped around 60 km without having to fight for it. At 1600hrs, they reached the Volga.**

The 16th Panzer Division's advance was so quick that its neighboring units, the 3rd and 60th Motorized Infantry Divisions, could not keep up and the armored division was alone when it reached the Volga. Luckily for the Germans, the Russians had been so taken by surprise by the speed of the enemy advance that they weren't able to form any effective opposition. Heavy anti-aircraft artillery opened fire in an impressive, but completely inefficient, barrage: the Russian pieces were silenced, one after the other, and the Germans discovered among the defenders' bodies the remains of women. These were workers from the Barrikady gun factory, who had been taught how to fire on enemy aircraft, but not how to fight against armored vehicles. Their sacrifice—made in vain—nevertheless showed that the Russians were ready to protect Stalingrad.

That day and the next, the Luftwaffe launched an unprecedented attack against Stalingrad. More than half of the bombs were incendiaries and the devastation was unimaginable: everything made of wood—which equated to entire blocks in Russian towns at the time—was set ablaze. The firestorm was vast and produced such smoke that some German soldiers swore they were only able to read a newspaper 60 kilometers away from Stalingrad. A soldier from the 267th Infantry Regiment, 94th Infantry Division, wrote his family a letter saying: "The whole city is on fire; under the Führer's orders, our Luftwaffe has made a huge blaze. It was necessary to end the Russian resistance."

The city had not been evacuated, and so was still home to around half a million civilians, who were subjected to the Luftwaffe's "terror bombing." Moreover, the consequences of the bombing were not wholly in the Germans' favor: fallen buildings obstructed the roads, which aided the defenders. The Allies experienced similar difficulties following ill-considered bombing raids at Monte Cassino, at Caen, and at The Hague. At the end of August, Hitler

Sixth Army
Rinok
VOLGA
Orlovka
Spartakovka
Gorodishche
Goumrak
Aleksandrovka
62nd Army
SOUTHEASTERN FRONT
Tsaritsa
Mamaev Kourgan
Fourth Panzer Army
Krasnoia Sloboda
Minina
Kouporosnoie
64th Army
Beketovka
Front line 12 Sept 1942
Limit of German advance
German attacks

On the outskirts of Stalingrad, the wreck of a T-34/76D offers shelter to a German machine-gun nest. The MG 34 is mounted on a heavy stand. Taking the city was going to be hugely difficult, and Paulus was nervous. (Bundesarchiv)

told Halder how the civilian population at Stalingrad should be treated: "Male population to be wiped out; female population to be exiled."[4]

In Moscow, anxiety was high: Stalin hadn't received any radio messages from Stalingrad for nearly 48 hours, and suspected the city had already been captured by the enemy. Finally, Vasilevsky managed to renew radio contact, and when Stalin heard the news that the Germans had reached the Volga, his reaction was such that Vasilevsky would never forget it, at least according to a 1965 article in the historical journal *Voenno Istoricheski Zhurnal.*

The situation, though difficult, was not as desperate as Stalin had imagined. In effect, the passage that the 16th Panzer Division had managed to open up was just three kilometers wide and 50 long, and it seemed like every artillery piece the Russians owned was firing on it night and day. Once again, Paulus was worried, and his anxiety was so obvious that von Richthofen even wrote about it in his personal journal:

> **August 25th, 1942. V.R. went by plane to the 76th Infantry Division, where he found Seydlitz and Paulus. Tense situation due to the impossibility of engaging reinforcements. The infantry was stopped left and right and was in no fit state to support the tanks that were largely outpacing the men. They are not going to be able to do it in three days. The situation has left Paulus visibly nervous. From 1300hrs, a massive aerial attack on Stalingrad, where fires are breaking out all over the place.**
>
> **August 27th, 1942. Paulus's spirits are low. Nothing particular happening on the front. Paulus and Hoth do not intend attacking before the 29th. V.R. sent the head of his Third Bureau to Jeschonnek and Marshal Goering to warn them that the army is nervous and that there are weaknesses within the command!**

4 Halder, Franz. *Kriegstagebuch: tägliche Aufzeichnungen des Chefs des Generalstabes des Heeres, 1939-1942*, Volume 3. Stuggart: W. Kohlhammer, 1964, p. 514.

The tanks' progress through the city was far from easy, and 16th Panzer Division was totally isolated at the beginning of the battle. (Bundesarchiv)

Fighting in the neighborhoods around Stalingrad. For the first time since the beginning of the war, the Germans used trenches. (Bundesarchiv)

This photograph could have been taken in North Africa, so desert-like is the landscape. The half-track is an SdKfz 10 carrying a 20mm Flak gun. (Bundesarchiv)

Paulus's nervousness was essentially due to the advanced position of the 16th Panzer Division, which was suffering greatly and could only be replenished at night by armored convoys. He was impatiently waiting for the Fourth Panzer Army's attack, but the latter was still making its way through the extensively mined sector north of Tinguta. After several days, Hoth gave up, and renewed his attack from a point somewhat further from Stalingrad. This allowed him to surprise the Soviets with his XXXXVIII Panzer Corps on August 31. The 24th Panzer Division arrived at a point 30 kilometers from Stalingrad on that same day, which had immediate consequences: the 62nd and 64th Armies, who had fought with dogged perseverance until that point, suddenly withdrew and abandoned their ground to retreat into the defensive lines closer to the city. On the evening of September 2, the units of Sixth Army and the Fourth Panzer Army joined up, but could not approach Stalingrad, as the Soviet resistance—to the north as well as to the south of the city—was so strong.

The Panzer III Ausf. Js of 2nd Battalion, 24th Panzer Regiment, 24th Panzer Division reached Stalingrad and enlarged the German bridgehead on the banks of the Volga. The city extended in a long, fairly straight band along the Volga. (Bundesarchiv)

An sIG 33 howitzer in action on the front at Stalingrad. Given its size, it is hard to see how it fitted whole—wheels and all—onto the small chassis of a Panzer I. (Bundesarchiv)

German soldiers engaged in fierce street fighting before they arrived in the suburbs of Stalingrad. The Russians were entrenched on every block, in every factory. This Heer officer is armed with a Soviet automatic gun. (Bundesarchiv)

# Afterword

The rapid retreat of 62nd and 64th Soviet Armies raised the hopes of German command, but it quickly became apparent they had underestimated their enemy, and that taking Stalingrad would not be easy. The Soviet forces had not abandoned Stalingrad to barricade themselves in on the east bank of the Volga. A coordinated, large-scale attack would be necessary to break through the Soviet defenses, as the defenders were going to put up one hell of a fight.

Nonetheless, Paulus and Hoth believed that if they acted without delay, before the city could be properly fortified, they could take Stalingrad quickly. Heavy bombing raids of the city continued and the city was quickly turned to rubble.

Both the Germans and the Russians both now faced a race against the clock: the Germans to regroup their troops for a final attack, and the Soviets to rebuild a coherent front capable of defending the city of Stalingrad. Stalin rushed available troops to bolster the city's defenses from as far away as Siberia, while the besieged citizens of Stalingrad were put to work building defensive works.

The resulting clash would be the single largest, and costliest, battle in the history of warfare.

German infantrymen were forced to cross the trenches to progress step-by-step towards the center of Stalingrad. (Bundesarchiv)

# Further Reading

Alexander, Christine and Mason Kunze (ed.). *Eastern Inferno: The Journals of a German Panzerjäger on the Eastern Front, 1941–1943*. Philadelphia: Casemate, 2011.

Beevor, Anthony. *Stalingrad*. New York: Viking, 1998.

Bergström, Christer. *Operation Barbarossa 1941: Hitler against Stalin*. Philadelphia: Casemate, 2016.

Clark, Alan. *Barbarossa: The Russian German Conflict 1941–1945*. London: Weidenfeld & Nicolson, 1995.

Cony, Christophe and Jean-Louis Roba. *Luftwaffe in Colour: From Glory to Defeat, 1942–45*. Philadelphia: Casemate, 2017.

Forczyk, Robert. *Kharkov 1942: The Wehrmacht strikes back*. Oxford: Osprey, 2013.

Forczyk, Robert. *Tank Warfare on the Eastern Front 1941–1942: Schwerpunkt*. Barnsley: Pen & Sword, 2014.

Glantz, David M. *Kharkov: Anatomy of a Military Disaster Through Soviet Eyes*. Ian Allan, 1998.

Halder, Franz. *Kriegstagebuch: tägliche Aufzeichnungen des Chefs des Generalstabes des Heeres, 1939–1942*, Volume 3. Stuggart: W. Kohlhammer, 1964.

Lemay, Benoît. *Erich von Manstein: Hitler's Master Strategist*. Philadelphia: Casemate, 2011.

These two men are unrolling a telephone wire in a ruined quarter of Stalingrad. The Luftwaffe raids caused enormous destruction that actually hindered the attackers, instead favoring the defenders of the city. (Bundesarchiv)

# Index